STEP-BY-STEP
ADVERTISING

STEP-BY-STEP
ADVERTISING

Cynthia S. Smith

S Sterling Publishing Co. Inc. New York
Distributed in the U.K. by Blandford Press

Library of Congress Cataloging in Publication Data
Smith, Cynthia S.
  Step-by-step advertising.

  Rev. ed. of: How to get big results from a small
advertising budget. 1973.
  Includes index.
  1. Advertising. I. Smith, Cynthia S. How to get
big results from a small advertising budget. II. Title.
HF5823.S619   1984   659.1   84-8455
ISBN 0-8069-0262-0
ISBN 0-8069-7852-X (pbk.)

Copyright © 1984, 1973 by Cynthia S. Smith
Published by Sterling Publishing Co., Inc.
Two Park Avenue, New York, N.Y. 10016
First edition published by Hawthorn Books, Inc.,
under the title "How to Get Big Results from
a Small Advertising Budget"
Distributed in Australia by Oak Tree Press Co., Ltd.
P.O. Box K514 Haymarket, Sydney 2000, N.S.W.
Distributed in the United Kingdom by Blandford Press
Link House, West Street, Poole, Dorset BH15 ILL, England
Distributed in Canada by Oak Tree Press Ltd.
c/o Canadian Manda Group, P.O. Box 920, Station U
Toronto, Ontario, Canada M8Z 5P9
Manufactured in the United States of America
All rights reserved

*Again, to my three VIP's:
David Smith, Hillary Smith, and Sarah Solondz*

CONTENTS

Introduction — 11

1 "Advertising! — 13
I know I need it, but what do I do?"

2 Do-It-Yourself Market Research — 16
How to know before you go

Interrogating the boss ... Where to pick up valuable marketing facts ... Research—by the numbers ... Attitudinal research—the focus group

3 The Budget — 37
Where to spend it

4 Media Selection — 39
Putting your money where the markets are

Which trade publications to pick ... How to listen to space salesmen ... Direct response ... Where to put your money

... What size ad? ... Timing: when to advertise ... Consumer magazine advertising ... Cooperative advertising

5 Purchasing Techniques 56

The trauma of buying intangibles

Glossary of ad terms ... How to tell good from bad when buying advertising services ... To bargain or not to bargain ... Avoiding shameful waste ... The "new corporate image" craze

6 Copywriting 69

How to write an ad that sells

Small and honest ... How to write copy that sells ... Supplementary copywriting tips

7 Direct Mail 78

The "now" medium

The familiar object in the unfamiliar place ... The bold fold ... The envelope for instant impact ... How to use color ... Newsletters—the personal touch ... Business-reply cards

8 Public Relations 94

How to write a news release

P.R. serves the media ... How to prepare a news release ... What should be publicized ... How to use P.R. to open new markets ... How to make news when nothing is happening ... Sundry P.R. suggestions

9 Radio 109
The one-to-one medium

10 Visual Sales Presentations 113
The invaluable selling tool

How to prepare a budget-version visual presentation ... Analyzing the sales story ... Using your presentation effectively

11 Trade Shows 122
Bringing in the buying bodies

Selecting the right exhibit display for your needs ... Furnishing your booth smartly ... Distribute literature, not catalogs ... Giveaways ... How to pull in selected traffic ... Show-time hints ... Hospitality suites

12 Sales Meetings 133
Love 'em and lead 'em

Love and catharsis for salesmen ... Planning the sales meeting ... Speakers—how to keep the meeting moving ... The secrets of smooth speech writing

13 The Secret of a Successful Catalog — 144

The buying/selling tool

How to plan and organize the catalog ... How to design the catalog ... How to mail the catalog ... How to cut down on errors and costs

14 Writing a Sales Letter — 160

How to get readership and response

The surefire four-step system for successful sales and letters ... Colors, paper, and personalizing

15 Point-of-Purchase Displays — 172

The selling moment of truth

How to know when you need a display ... Types of displays available ... The no-risk way of buying displays ... Promote your P.O.P. ... How to be sure your display keeps on selling

Index — 185

INTRODUCTION

About ten years ago, a friend of mine was on a vacation in Jamaica where he struck up a casual conversation with a man on the adjacent lounge chair at the beach.

"What business are you in?" my friend asked.

"Advertising," answered the gentleman.

"Oh really?" said my friend. "Did you ever hear of C/D Smith Advertising Agency?"

While recounting the story to me later, my friend said smugly, "Well, when the guy said he never heard of you, I figured he wasn't very big in the advertising business."

"Did you get the man's name?" I asked.

"Oh yes. His name was Bernbach—Bill Bernbach—I think."

Since Doyle Dane Bernbach, Inc. is one of the biggest ad agencies in the country, and Bill Bernbach a virtual legend, the story seemed quite humorous to me at the time. But things have changed in the past ten years. Today, small ad agencies have assumed a position of importance as suppliers to small business, that burgeoning segment of the American economy. Recent statistics recognize the small business as a major factor in the national economic growth.

Starting and building and running a small business is an exhilarating—albeit exasperating—experience. In today's computerized, impersonal world, it's the only frontier left for rugged individuals who want to exercise some control over their own destinies and time. But like all small enterprises, it requires a comprehensive array of talents and abilities not demanded in big business where you are deposited into a one-dimensional slot and develop your skills in that one area. In small business, you have no resource but *you*. There are no departments to call

When you need advice on marketing, no specialists to dial on the intercom when you want to talk about P.R. It's all *you* and you'd better know what to do and when.

It's great to be a big fish in a small pond. It's sensational to be able to make your own creative decisions about marketing and sales promotion without having to defend and rationalize your opinions for a committee. It's downright exciting to get an idea and personally see it through without being deterred by endless and usually pointless meetings. (Did you ever notice that whenever you phone employees of large companies, eight out of ten times they're "in a meeting"? What on earth do they all talk about?)

I have always found it amusing to hear the condescension accorded the small-budget advertiser by inhabitants of the big ad agencies. They entertain themselves with the myth that only dropouts from Madison Avenue and ad folks who have been jettisoned when they hit the over-the-hill age of 40 work in the small ad field as a last resort before the skids. They really believe that any talented titan of the 4A's could walk into a small company, feed them an economy version of one of their million-dollar campaigns, and score a smasheroo. What a bust! In fact, these narrowly trained experts would bomb out in a flash. It's happened time and again, because handling the advertising of a small business requires a knowledge and grasp of the whole picture. You must understand marketing, research, media, graphics, direct mail, copywriting, point of purchase, packaging, public relations, etc. You must be able to perform all of these jobs or know where and how to buy the talent to perform them.

For over 15 years, I have been dealing with, lecturing to, and writing books and columns on advertising and public relations for people in small business. I have been teaching a two-day seminar entitled *How to Get Big Results from a Small Advertising Budget* to executives, company presidents, and marketing people under the aegis of the continuing education divisions of 32 universities throughout the United States. And everywhere I go, reactions are the same: "I've gotten more usable ideas from this seminar than I picked up from all the courses and books I've taken and read before." Of course, in order to teach small business people you have to understand the nature of small business. Theory? Who has time to learn theory? Tactics and usable ideas—that's what counts.

This book is neither a tome of theory nor a complicated discussion on methodologies. It's a guide to effective, low-cost, practical promotions and campaigns and advertising and P.R. ideas that you can put into use *today*. So read it—and then go forth and conquer!

"ADVERTISING! 1
I know I need it, but what do I do?"

Sure, you mean to get to work on your advertising, as soon as you get a moment. You know that advertising, publicity, and sales promotion are prime business-builders, and when properly done, can make the difference between profit and loss. However, in any small business your days are so filled with the millions of minute details that crop up; you are so involved in handling crises and problems that demand immediate attention—like paying bills, meeting payroll, checking on lost shipments, filling in for absent personnel—that finding time to work on advance planning for your advertising is a luxury you never seem to achieve.

So, most of your advertising money goes into "Gotta" advertising. What's "Gotta" advertising? It's the usually ineffective promotions you got roped into by aggressive, eager space salesmen who call with that urgent tone that is an occupational characteristic, saying, "We're having a *Special Section* in the next issue devoted to *your* products and/or your locality. All your competitors will probably be in. Of course, you've *gotta* be in!"

Since you never have time to study the situation, and he plays on the secret fear that lies within the breast of every business person—that the competition knows something you don't—you agree to take an ad and allow the publication's ad department to prepare an ad for you which will inevitably be neat, undramatic and unproductive. What does their staff know about your merchandising features? A month later, another space salesman hits you with the same "you've *gotta* be in" pitch. Maybe this time it's for a local organization's souvenir journal and you bite again. Then the end of the year comes and your accountant presents you with figures showing that you spent thousands of dollars for advertising, and you shriek, "For *what?*"

Indeed, for what? You have expended precious dollars and probably derived precious little from the expenditure. It is at this point you realize that taking the time to plan your advertising is no longer a luxury; it is a necessity.

Maybe you are the sales manager, or office manager, or salesperson for a small company and the company just sort of grew. No one was ever designated to handle advertising. Then one day that urgent call comes from the "Gotta" advertising space salesman, and your boss looks at you and says, "Didn't you say you took a course in advertising in college?" Or maybe he says, "Say, that was a cute poem you wrote for Joe's birthday party last week. You're pretty creative." Before you know it, you have been made responsible for the preparation of an ad. It turns out fairly well, and from that point on, everything pertaining to advertising, sales promotion, and public relations is turned over to you. Suddenly you are the de facto advertising manager of the company—without the title and probably without the salary.

Perhaps you have or are planning to start a small mail order business—as a new enterprise or as an adjunct to an existing establishment. Since mail order is based totally on advertising—there's no store for buyers to visit and no salespeople to convince them—the ads must do the entire job. Then you must become knowledgeable about media buying (where to run your ads), good product photography (the picture must be detailed and enticing enough to make them desire it desperately), and alluring copywriting (strong enough to induce them to send in money). You know you must become adept in all these vital areas if your business is to succeed, but how can you accomplish this when your days are so jammed?

That's what this book is about. It will give you the basic rudiments of all areas of advertising and sales promotion from the unique point of view of the moderate-budget advertiser. It will familiarize you with the terminology and procedures required to create effective advertising programs for your company—*on a realistic budget*. It will teach you how to develop the overview required of all small business advertising people, because the big business advertising luxury of departmentalized chores is not for the likes of us.

"ADVERTISING! I KNOW I NEED IT, BUT WHAT DO I DO?"

You will learn to develop advertising antennae, the turned-on awareness that directs you to seek and spot the promotional publicizable possibilities of occurrences that are going on around you. If there's any single secret to success in advertising, that's it—the ability to recognize special marketing opportunities as they arise, and, of course, the skill and knowledge to act effectively.

That's just what you will learn in this book. The few hours you invest in reading it will set you up forever as an ad man or ad woman. If you are the owner of a small business and must do your own advertising, this book will equip you to handle it easily, creatively and, most importantly, economically. You will learn ways to get $100 worth of advertising out of every ten dollars you spend.

Do-It-Yourself Market Research   2

How to know before you go

It has a forbidding ring to it: "Market Research." It conjures up images of questionnaires, computers and big costs. But it's really quite simple. Market research is merely the quest for information about your customer. Who is most likely to want your product or service, when, and why?

Market research is the basic step that must be taken before you make any advertising move. It will enable you to target markets so that you put your bucks where the buyers are. What is the point of advertising in a publication that reaches one million people—no matter how much of a bargain price it seems—when only two thousand readers are potential customers for your products or services? You must do market research in order to ascertain exactly what sort of people have been or should be buying your products, so that you can seek out the publications that reach that exact group.

Important facts like peak vs. poor selling periods and regional preferences for specific products must be considered before you arrive at any intelligent advertising program.

Now, where and how can you find all this valuable data without investing a fortune with some high-ticket market research company? It's simple, thanks to a proven system I have developed.

INTERROGATING THE BOSS

Okay, let's begin. You want to uncover the full picture of the company's existing and potential marketing situation. Before you can move into planning, you must be fully aware of its weaknesses and strengths. In the absence of computerized data, I have evolved a very simple method of eliciting the basic facts. It's not as scientific as one might like, but over the years it has proven surprisingly exact. It's called "interrogating the boss."

The term "boss" is a loosely applied one. It's the person in charge—usually the one who founded the firm or built it up to its present position. His or her head contains most of the data you need, but it takes judicious questioning and interpreting to sift out the accurate information. (If *you* are the boss, it will be slightly tougher, but try to be objective.)

Beware of the following pitfalls. Remember that this individual's opinions are often based on judgments made when he was last out in the field—which could be 20 years ago. So listen for the facts, and ignore the judgments. Remember, too, that he has been so wrapped up in the company that his vision is frequently clouded by proprietary feelings that tend to cloud his objectivity. For example, he will undoubtedly refer to his company as pioneers or leaders in the industry. I have yet to encounter a small company president who did not state this conviction with great emphasis and pride. Never mind that. I figure that anyone who has succeeded in the onerous task of building a company is entitled to that conceit—he's earned it; but I do mind when they express a deep conviction that their customers really care. It's often hard to convince them that nobody really gives much of a damn what your company contributed to the industry 15 years ago—or 15 hours ago, for that matter. Customers deal with now, and so must we.

Now that you are fully prepared for the pitfalls, have the boss sit down, arm yourself with pen and pad, and ask away.

In Which Market Are Company Products Now Being Sold?

Possible answers might be in terms of *Economic* markets (such as, having an art gallery and realizing that most of the paintings are bought by persons making $50,000 a year and over, whereas the lithographs and prints are going primarily to those making $20,000 a year and under). They might be in terms of *Professions* (an insurance broker might find that higher-cost annuity policies are bought primarily by doctors, whereas straight life policies are preferred by lawyers). There could be *Trade* markets (a pencil manufacturer or distributor of specialized types of pencils that go to architects, artists, accountants, and so on).

Then there are *Geographic* markets. If you have a retail shop, are your customers just from the immediate area or do you draw from neighboring towns? If you are in a shopping mall, perhaps many of your customers are transients. If you are in a resort area, tourists may make up a large portion of your patronage. Is it suburban, rural, or urban people who comprise the bulk of your market?

Perhaps you sell a product that has only regional appeal, such as sailboats—you wouldn't expect them to sell as well in landlocked areas as in coastal regions, nor would you expect water softeners to sell in cities where the need doesn't exist.

How about *Age* markets? Does your product or service appeal to teenagers, young marrieds, senior citizens? If your store is located in a Sun Belt community, you are certain to have a patronage drawn from the senior citizen category.

In Which Other Markets Do You Think These Products Could Be Sold?

Here you can come up with some imaginative lulus. But take note, and distill practical reality from unrealistic thinking. Beware of the situation like that of the manufacturer who put one of his small industrial soda fountains (which retailed for only $5,000) in his playroom bar and believed that there was a large potential market for it for home use. There's a thread of an idea here, but you certainly couldn't accept his forecast for a mass-market potential without doing a lot of further investigation.

What Are the Current Methods of Distribution?

Company salesmen: These are people employed solely by the company and paid directly by them. This is the best setup from a sales promotional point of view, because company salesmen are the most cooperative and responsive. They have to be—their jobs depend on it. They can be counted on to distribute advertising material, to follow up sales leads, to see that counter and window displays are set up when and where you want.

Manufacturers' representatives: This is usually an organization of two or more individuals who represent many companies in allied fields. They are independent agents who sell the products of a number of companies, usually of a related category that can be sold to the same outlets. They are paid commission for what they sell. The company handles billing and shipping.

Representatives are harder to handle and present more of a challenge to creators of sales promotional material. For one thing, they are independent entrepreneurs, and although your company's line is important to them, they are not totally dependent; yours is just one of many. This means you won't be able to issue orders or make heavy demands on their time. Their sales technique involves a quick hit-and-run in each outlet they call on. In the maybe ten minutes' time the buyer allots them, they must show and sell perhaps a dozen different products. So they are not likely to want to use any of that valuable time for any nonselling activity, such as setting up displays or talking up advertising campaigns. Also, they will not carry any cumbersome material. If you have ever gone around with any of these salesmen and watched them lug in cases of samples and selling literature, you would appreciate their reluctance to add further burdens.

So when you find that you are dealing with a manufacturer's rep, be aware of the natural limitations, and prepare your material accordingly.

Wholesale distributors: These are companies that buy merchandise from many firms and resell it to small outlets. They are middlemen, in effect, who stock, ship, and bill and who employ their own salesmen.

This method of distribution means the least amount of advertising cooperation. It means that the ultimate seller of your products has no contact with your company; he deals only with the wholesaler. The wholesaler's salesman has no loyalty to you at all—his salary comes from the wholesaler.

Is the Company Satisfied with Its Sales in Each Territory?

You undoubtedly will learn that some areas are weaker in sales than others. It is vital that you analyze why. There are two common answers: poor salesmen and difficult territory.

Poor salesmen: You will be told that slow sales in a specific area are due to the ineptness of the local salesmen. That may or may not be true. It's important that you check this out; the results will determine areas of advertising expenditure. Find out if other salesmen who previously covered that territory fared better under the same conditions. If the salesman is a manufacturer's rep who sells other companies' products, does he perform equally poorly for them? If you have, in fact, a rotten sales force in the area and it cannot be replaced readily, you will have to plan some hard-hitting local campaigns to help it along.

Difficult territory: The other standard complaint—that one territory is particularly difficult—may have some validity. If you're selling Toyotas, you won't expect too wild a response in Detroit.

What you have to watch for here are *excuses* instead of reasons. After a while you can develop the ability to detect what psychiatrists call the emotional sound of truth. You will hear the false ring of an excuse. Here are two of the oldest sales-failure bromides of them all: "They only buy from buddies down there." The gist of this theory is that a fierce regional loyalty exists in the area and that only local boys can make good there. Nonsense. I've heard this one over and over again and found it phony every time. True, a customer may prefer to buy from a buddy, but business is business. Give a buyer a profit-making product or an item that pleases him more than someone else's and he'll buy yours over his brother's. Money creates a unique selfishness; the desire to get the best for the money transcends all emotional considerations.

"Competition has the area all sewn up." This may or may not be so. Before you accept it as gospel, be aware that businessmen usually have an overblown image of how well their competitors are doing. This reasoning is usually a compound of jealousy plus the assumption that, "If we're not getting the business, someone else must be." Sometimes, however, no one has really tapped the full potential of an area. The only way to find the facts is to pay a visit to the area. See as many buyers as you can. Ask questions, and look around; you may find the most amazing reasons for sluggish sales.

I was once assured by a manufacturer's representative that the entire city of Cleveland was off limits for our line of products because, whereas he was based in Chicago and could get to Cleveland only a few times a year, the competitor had a resident salesman in the city. How could he compete with a salesman who dropped in on the dealers every week?

I went out there to look the situation over. And I found out that in one respect he was right: The competitor did have a resident salesman in Cleveland, an elderly semiretired gentleman who had little to do, handled just the one line, and enjoyed visiting the dealers often. But I also discovered that the storekeepers did not take pleasure in his frequent visits. They found him a pain in the neck who demanded too much of their valuable time. Even more important, I noticed that although they did buy all of that category of merchandise from the competitor, all that they bought was not nearly enough for a city like Cleveland. There was very little on the shelves, and none displayed. Obviously there was some weakness in the selling presentation.

Just a little questioning of the buyers, the salespeople, and the store managers quickly indicated the low importance they assigned to the entire product category. Obviously they considered it a minor line with limited appeal.

The situation was quite simple to remedy. All that had to be done was to mount a city-wide sales promotion and advertising campaign. The promotion produced a volume of demand that the dealers never knew existed. It showed that they had been overlooking a valuable source of sales—a situation they were most eager to rectify, of course. From that point on, they began to buy the whole line in a depth unprecedented for Cleveland, featuring it on counters and in windows—and selling. Another important side benefit was the attitude of our company's manufacturer's representative. He learned that he could indeed sell in a city he had long since given up. The experience taught him never to yield a territory under those conditions again.

What are your goals and objectives? Where do you plan to be next year, and within the next two years? Every business must have a specific direction and goal so that you can map out an effective route. Unfortunately, many small businesses regard the setting of tangible objectives as blue-sky theory that conflicts with the seat-of-the-pants methods they have been using with some success for years. That old-style "let's-just-watch-the-bottom-line-and-never-mind-how-we-get-there" technique cannot survive in today's computer-oriented and highly competitive business environment. Just taking sales as they come without any investigation or analysis of their sources and causes and then using that information to plot the future directions, is an invitation to eventual failure.

What new markets do you plan to enter and approximately when? What share of the market should you realistically seek? The operative word here is "realistically." Too many business people believe they should have 100 percent of the market and are driven to a doomed-from-the-start goal. No one company can get 100 percent of any market. For years, the advertising agencies that Alka-Seltzer® employed turned out outstanding television campaigns that were memorable and effective. Yet Alka-Seltzer would switch from agency to agency. Why? Because they sought to increase their sales to an unrealistic percentage of the existing market. There will always be people who prefer the pink creaminess of Pepto-Bismol® to the effervescent fizz of Alka-Seltzer, and attempting to convert these folks can only lead to lots of wheel-spinning and a waste of money.

Just remember that there are two basic ways to increase sales: (1) Extract more business from your current customers. (2) Open new markets and create new customers. A healthy business works on both goals simultaneously and consistently.

AFTER INTERROGATING THE BOSS

Now that you have picked the boss's brain clean, it's time to move on to another ranking member of the firm, with the same bank of questions. It might be the sales manager, general manager, sometimes even the head bookkeeper. In small companies you frequently run into situations where an unspecified individual with no discernible title turns out to be the one who really runs the show. It's easy to identify this person. When you are questioning the boss, if more than three times he counters your question with, "Wait, I'll ask Charlie," then you know that Charlie's your man. Get to him next, and ask him exactly the same questions you have asked his employer. It is vital to have his more objective, less emotional point of view, as a backup check of the facts you have already accumulated.

Now that you have accumulated all the information, you have a picture of how, where, and what the company sells. You are prepared to plan a marketing strategy that will be aimed at remedying the weaknesses and exploiting the strengths you have discovered.

WHERE TO PICK UP VALUABLE MARKETING FACTS

Trade Publications

Every industry has its share of trade publications. It's their business to have statistics on the buying and selling habits of the industry. And this valuable information is yours for the asking. For instance, they can usually supply you with a listing of the peak selling months in your industry, plus a geographic breakdown of the largest consumption areas in the country.

Think of how invaluable that can be. Suppose your questioning has turned up the fact that sales in the Southwest dropped last year. Then the trade publication's survey figures show that area enjoyed a remarkable general upsurge in sales last year, possibly due to new industry or new marketing awareness in the territory. Obviously, something is very wrong in your sales department.

Perhaps you learn that most people in the industry do very poorly in summer, and your company does fantastically well in those months. Such a disparity rings an alarm bell. Find out what you are doing right. Perhaps you are doing something different in June, July, and August. Check. You may discover a sales technique that you can apply successfully the rest of the year. You can learn a great deal from successes as well as from failures.

As an example, *Jewelers' Circular Keystone,* the major magazine in the jewelry industry, has a market research department that is happy to tell you how many people in the Southwest bought wristwatches in various price brackets during the past year. If you are a retailer in that area, this information can guide your purchasing plans for price lines of watches. If you are a watch manufacturer, you now have an understanding of the potential regional reception for your price products.

Without this sort of information, you might have made a disastrous decision. If you decided that San Antonio is not a major hub of prosperity and it did not pay to promote your line of $700 to $2,000 watches there, you would have missed out on a million dollar market opportunity. A check of the high-priced watch sales figures in San Antonio before the devaluation of the peso showed that millions of dollars worth of high-priced watches were sold annually to the suddenly oil-rich Mexicans who crossed the border regularly to avail themselves of the lavish jewelry they could buy in the United States at so-called bargain prices.

The most important thing about trade publications is their active desire to help companies in their industry. I have great faith in altruism, but there's nothing like the profit motive to get guys off their butts to give you immediate action. True, there's a lot of information you can pick up from government pamphlets, but did you ever try to get fast action from a government employee?

If you want to break into a new field and want to set up a sales force, the trade-publication space salesman will gladly help you do so. He knows that once you prepare to introduce your products to a new field, you will want to advertise to reach the potential buyers, and that will mean advertising billing for him. It's a very open relationship—one hand washing the other, and all that. You don't have to make any false promises or commitments. Any space salesman worth his salt knows he must invest a certain amount of his time in cultivating potential customers, and he'll give you all the marketing and promotion help he can.

The publications usually have a list of all the salesmen and manufacturers' sales representatives and wholesale distributors in the industry. They also usually know who's good, who's eager, who's looking for new lines, and will gladly steer you to the right sales organization.

Take advantage of the services and cooperation offered by the trade publications; it can be invaluable.

Read your trade publications carefully. You will find a wealth of information in them. Clip and collect competitors' ads and publicity as well as your own. Develop a "swipe file" (more properly called a reference file); it's always handy to know what everyone else is doing.

Another important source of marketing data is your *trade association*. Every industry has an organization whose sole goal is to promote the image and ultimately the sales of that field. To fulfil that function, they must continually amass marketing information, trends, and figures that affect the industry. They are there to be tapped.

Local chambers of commerce are great places to find facts about local conditions and business operations in the area. Suppose you plan to open a computer store in a specific locality. Before you decide what sorts of software to stock, you must know the kinds of businesses that exist in the areas you plan to reach. Are there predominantly small businesses in the area? Does it seem to be heavy in certain types of businesses, i.e., auto body shops, professional buildings, large corporate headquarters? Check with the chamber of commerce for a listing of local industry.

If you are interested in the total subject of market research, a good reference guide you can obtain free from the government would be:

> MARKETING RESEARCH PROCEDURES
> Small Business Bibliography #9
> Small Business Administration
> Washington, DC 20416

Company Salesmen

Salesmen are the central intelligence banks of the business world. Treat them with consideration and loving care, and you'll turn up the hottest market research information you can hope for.

These people are out in the market, in the field, on the battle lines every day. They are continually in contact with the buyers and the buying public. The only thing you must also realize is that few of them are at all aware of the valuable information they carry. It's up to you to pry it loose.

It's not hard. They respond eagerly to simple consideration and attentiveness. You must understand that these folks are out all day taking guff, rudeness, and rebuffs. Then they come back to the home office and are bawled out for not selling enough or not checking properly on someone's credit. Or they learn that the order they sweated over for two months, nurturing a customer to develop him into an account, cannot be shipped for another four weeks. They are loaded with gripes, and there's no place to unburden them. Let your office become the unburdening depot, and you'll turn up a wealth of goodies, as well as making life easier for these heroic men of the road.

What sort of things can you learn? You can discover new and unusual uses for your company's products and what kind of displays are needed at the point of purchase. All sorts of ideas come out when you give salesmen a chance to talk to you about their experiences.

A good way to get them started is to mention the specific success of another salesman. Salesmen by nature are garrulous and somewhat egotistical, and someone else's success always prods them. For instance, you might open with "I hear Dave Johnson is selling that little machine light to sewing-machine manufacturers by the thousands. Great idea, isn't it?" Inevitably, he'll come up with a parallel unusual application that he uncovered—some sale he has made that could open an entirely new marketing outlet.

Minds run in odd ways and need different sorts of stimuli. If you had asked him the direct question "Have you uncovered any unusual uses for this light?" he would undoubtedly have racked his brain for a moment and then come up empty. That's a thing to remember in all your do-it-yourself market research. *Never ask a direct question that invites a "yes" or "no" answer.* People are too ready to take the lazy way out and say no. Appeal to their egos, and you'll get action.

I once uncovered a gold mine by asking a salesman why he sold so few of the company's credit-card cases and wallet inserts. Stung to the quick by my casting aspersions on his selling ability, he came up with a quick answer that revolutionized and quadrupled the company's sales of that group of products: "Because it takes too damn long to sell all those little penny-ante plastic cases. It's nickel-and-dime stuff, and by the time the customer cherry-picks—'How many of these should I take? Is this a good mover? Maybe I should order twelve'—I've spent 15 minutes and ended up with a $50 sale! In that same amount of time, I could have sold the man ring binders at $20 a pop and racked up a $500 order. It just doesn't pay! Why don't you come up with a prepacked assortment of these cases that I could just walk in with and say, 'Look, here are the best items in the line all in one neat display'? I could sell the man the same $50 worth of stuff in two minutes."

It was such a great idea that I wondered why no one had thought of it before. That's usually the way; the obvious tends to be overlooked. I dashed out to the factory on the spot and we put together a mock-up display assortment of the cases in quantities that the salesman felt were feasible. Six of this number, two dozen of that, and so on. I contacted a counter display maker, had a sample unit made in cardboard, and then presented it to my boss. And he called in our Vice-President in Charge of Objections.

You know the one—every business has one. That's the person who can be counted upon to come up with the largest range of negatives imaginable to any new project. I'm convinced those people are motivated by two qualities: sloth and envy. Sloth because something new means the status quo will be disturbed and they will undoubtedly be called upon to do something. Envy because you thought of it and they didn't. Anyway, this V.P. in Charge of No's reacted with his usual opening line: "Are you kidding?" in a voice ringing with a mix of contempt and ridicule. He proceeded to point out why few retailers would consider buying this nonsensical piece of point-of-purchase. I have learned never to get angry at these prognosticators of doom but to listen to all the dire caveats they predict. Sprinkled among the promised pitfalls could be a real factor that should be dealt with at the outset.

Never allow these doomsayers to deter you from a project that you believe in. I was finally begrudgingly permitted to order a minimum starting quantity. "Don't order more than 250. You'll be lucky if we move half." (Our customer list was 10,000.) To say that the unit was successful is a major understatement. The results were so astronomical that they are no longer measurable. It made such sense. Not only did it make the initial sale of the array of plastic card cases a cinch, but subsequent reorders became automatic. From the basic cardboard display, we moved into permanent metal. Today you will see the selfsame unit, unchanged after many years (why tamper with a good thing?), on the counters of stationery stores throughout the country. This was a classic case of picking up invaluable market information from an unsuspecting salesman.

Retail Salespeople

Who better knows what the customers want than the people who wait on them? Your own sales force is filled with marketing information, but they don't realize it. A wealth of knowledge is buried in their subconscious, and it is incumbent upon you to extract it. Remember that salespeople are intent on one objective when they are on the floor—to make the sale. They react to the customer and respond instantaneously based upon the demands of the situation. If the customer evinces specific needs, they try to come up with reasons why the product being shown fills that need to a tee. In the heat of battle, they never stop to examine the expressed needs and preferences. They just field questions as they arise and try to answer them in a positive way that will convince the customer to buy now. However, do you realize the valuable marketing information they are subconsciously accumulating? They actually know who's buying what and why—just the sort of data that would enable you to determine which markets to go after, and what sorts of merchandise to offer in those specific areas.

Have sales meetings at least once a week. In the morning before the store opens, or an evening after closing. Make it pleasant; serve coffee and danish; keep the atmosphere easy. The purpose of these meetings is to effect an exchange of information about what makes people buy. You must direct the meeting in a way that cajoles them into recalling details of sales they made which can serve to suggest new approaches to merchandising as well as advertising and selling. A "yes" or "no" question will get you nowhere: "Did any of you make an unusual sale last week?" will probably produce a large silence. Most salespeople are not tuned in to conceptual merchandising, and they undoubtedly do not realize that an unusual sale is one that involved a type of buyer who does not customarily enter your store, or a person who purchases a product for a unique application. The best way to evoke the sort of information you need is by appealing to their egos. "Did you all hear about that marvellous sale Mary made last week?" Then describe the elements of the transaction. That will sting the rest of your staff to their collective egos. To counteract your compliment to Mary and to extract equal approbation, everyone will try to come up with similar situations in which he, too, effected out-of-the-ordinary sales.

For example, a needlepoint store owner I know benefitted handsomely from an employee recounting at a sales meeting how a customer in a lower middle-class neighborhood announced that she was making a series of needlepoint hangings to provide a heritage for her children. As she put it, "I don't have expensive jewelry and things to leave to our kids, and I'd like them to have some mementos of me after I'm gone. I'm doing these needlepoint hangings so they have some heirlooms that they can pass on to their kids." The concept sparked a very successful ad campaign that bore the slogan, "You don't have to be wealthy to leave heirlooms."

Suppliers' Salespeople

Who would know more about what's going on in the industry than the people who spend their days moving from store to store, office to office, or factory to factory dealing with the key buying people in each organization. They're walking treasure troves of vital information, and they dearly love to disseminate it. They know who's doing well and who's not, and probably why. They know who's selling what, because their orders give them instant insights into the character and volume of business being enjoyed by every establishment they visit.

Use them. Question them. Find out what your competition is doing. Why is the store in a neighboring shopping mall selling so much of an item that you can't seem to move at all? Look at their advertising, check their store layout. You may find they have found a special merchandising approach that you can adopt to promote your profits.

Space Salesmen

Advertising salesmen for the trade magazines are people of real importance. More than anyone else, they know what's going on in the field—the facts, the rumors, the scuttlebutt. You'll find out where and when your competitors advertise and what markets they plan to enter. If you are looking for a job, by the way, or some key company personnel to fill a vacancy, these are the boys who can help. Just be friendly and hospitable, and keep your ears open. You'll soon find out who's doing what to whom and for how much, and other data that might come in handy.

And remember that these chaps adore gossip. That's their stock and trade. I find them faster at spreading news than native drums, and use them accordingly. If I have facts that I wish to convey to the industry quickly and I don't have the time or budget to do an ad or mailing, I just call on one of the space salesmen and casually drop the information, usually with the preamble: "Listen, this is confidential, so don't tell anyone—but here's what's happening here." You can reasonably expect the information to be around the entire industry within a week.

Order Clerks

The company order clerk—anyone who takes orders over the phone or processes the incoming written orders—is another local treasure of market data. Order clerks are aware of the ultimate destination of the company's products, since they see the shipping addresses on the orders. This can alert you to entirely new markets.

Ask them to advise you when they come across something out of the ordinary—an unusual destination, a type of company they are not accustomed to dealing with, an exotic locality they are not used to seeing. Ask every order clerk, "Have you come across any unusual uses for our products?" They will be most cooperative. The day of an order clerk can be mighty dreary. Any bit of creative spice you can impart is much appreciated. Also, it gives them a feeling of importance and involvement with the company's advertising program.

Just as an illustration of the sort of valuable information you can turn up in this way, let's go back to that manufacturer of soda-fountain equipment and that small soda-fountain unit he had installed in his home. An alert order clerk began to notice that one salesman was selling a number of these small units to hospitals, an unusual destination for this type of equipment. She advised us, and we contacted the salesman to learn his secret. It was a beaut. It seems that every hospital has a large number of restricted-diet patients on each floor who are not permitted the usual sugared soft drinks. The smart salesman sold hospitals on the idea of putting a small soda-fountain unit of sugar-free sodas on each floor where the nurse could draw drinks conveniently.

This little tip led to a whole advertising campaign to hospitals and the ultimate sale of thousands of dollars' worth of these units.

And then there was the order clerk for the company that produced linens for department stores and linen shops. Whenever I start with a new client, I seek out the order clerk and leave my card on her desk with the request to phone me whenever she comes across an unusual shipment. I always open with "Would you like to help in our marketing and advertising?" I find that in this anonymous computerized era we live in where people become numbers, everyone is hungry to be of consequence. Everyone wants to feel he can make some contribution, can gain the recognition and sense of self-importance that comes from doing something of importance. The order clerk, a lovely, shy middle-aged woman, phoned me one day. "I don't know if this is the sort of thing you mean, but one of our salesmen is selling a lot of satin pillowcases to beauty salons. Now we *never* sell to hairdressers, and I don't know what they're doing with them." I thanked her and phoned the salesman for an explanation of this bonanza he seemed to have discovered. This occurrence dates back to the sixties when teased hairdos were the rage. A woman would spend $20 to have her hair styled and teased so that every strand stood at attention, and then have to sleep standing up to preserve her coiffure because cotton pillowcases cause friction that disturbed the hair. But satin pillowcases presented no such problem. You might slide all over the bed at night, but your hairdo remained intact. This canny salesman knew that women were buying satin pillowcases in department and linen stores for just this purpose, and he suddenly got an idea: Why not offer coiffure-preservation insurance at the point of sale to women who have just invested $20 for a hairdo? Beauty salons customarily do a brisk business in related beauty items which are displayed in showcases at the cash register. So his introduction of packages of satin pillowcases into the shops was very simple.

It was a great marketing concept and opened a whole new, lucrative market for my client. We immediately sent letters to all the company salesmen to alert them to this great new potential sales outlet. Then we began sending direct mail to the beauty shops and advertising in their trade magazines. While the teased-hair craze lasted, the company enjoyed a marvellous new source of profits. And all from the observation of an order clerk.

RESEARCH—BY THE NUMBERS

Basically there are two types of market research techniques—*Numbers* and *Attitudinal*. *Numbers* research involves questionnaires and field work and big bucks. Haven't you ever been stopped at a shopping mall by a charming young woman equipped with pen and a questionnaire, and been taken through a series of questions pertaining to your attitudes about specific products—or been called on the phone, usually in the middle of dinner, by someone from a research organization who wishes to have a few moments of your time to answer questions? This is the numbers research procedure and you are but one of thousands of people they must interview to get valid results. This is a very costly procedure because of the large numbers involved. One of my clients, a manufacturer of expensive watches, spent $25,000 for a study to learn how many people recognized their brand, why people bought watches that cost $300 or more, who they were, and what motivated them to make their specific choices. The quantity of questionnaires ultimately produced and computed was not large. The big expense was the thousands of people who had to be phoned and qualified by interviewers in order to come up with the selective market they needed.

Numbers research requires lots of numbers because spot interviews are heavily affected by the interviewees' moods at the moment of questioning. If you are questioned by phone, and your husband has just called to say he won't be home for dinner and you have a soufflé standing by—or you are stopped by an interviewer at a mall just as you're walking to find a phone to summon help for your dead battery—chances are your emotional state will be somewhat rocky, which will certainly affect your answers. Thus, many, many questionnaires have to be evaluated to compensate for these potentials for inaccuracy.

I have had executives who attended my seminars announce proudly that they had performed market research studies: questionnaires sent to some selected customers, or 20 phone calls made to a specific area, or questionnaires that were left on store counters to be filled out by the whims of whomever. Or, "We did a survey of the man in the street—I asked my brother-in-law, the fellow from the deli who delivers danish, and the elevator operator. *They* liked the idea, so it must be good!"

It is downright dangerous to predicate any costly business decision based on such an inadequate, sloppy, and unscientific procedure. Numbers research must be done in sufficient quantities, with proper selection processing, experienced interviewers, and most importantly, a questionnaire prepared by a highly skilled and experienced individual. To extract the information you need, questions have to be developed that get to the true heart of the matter. And to be sure that the answers you evoke are reflective of the interviewees' true feelings, questions have to be framed very carefully.

This is no arena for amateurs. Numbers research had best be left for the big spenders. But fear not. There *is* a technique used by the billion-dollar companies that is simple and inexpensive enough to be used by even the smallest business.

It's called Focus Groups.

ATTITUDINAL RESEARCH—THE FOCUS GROUP

Someone in the company has come up with what looks like a great idea for a product. Everyone thinks it has potential, but how can you be sure, before you put thousands into production, that it will sell? And, further, how do you know which aspects of the new product are the most appealing to the buying public?

In other words, is there a big enough need for it to justify the investment? And, if so, what will be the prime motivation for someone to buy it?

Maybe you'd like to rearrange your store to give it a new image, or install a totally new kind of department. Before you make the major investment that such changes necessitate, wouldn't you like to find out if your concept is justified, if people will respond to the "new look," if the new lines and new department will bring in enough traffic to justify the expense?

Fortunately, it's possible to get some answers to these vital questions before you make the big plunge, by using a focus group.

A focus group is actually a microcosm of your market, brought together in one room for a sort of consciousness-raising session discussion about your product or service.

Led by a moderator, the participants respond to a series of questions, which are aimed at evoking emotions and reactions. It's called *attitudinal* research because you are able to deal with whole attitudes rather than just spot responses. And it's invaluable because you not only learn *what* they think of your product or service, but *why*.

The procedure is simple. Here are the guidelines:

Type of group: Be selective but random about whom you gather. If you are testing a consumer product, be sure you have people who will be in the proper purchasing power group for that item. In other words, don't question Fifth Avenue matrons about men's work clothes. If it's a product that will be bought by both men and women, have representatives of both sexes. Ascertain that you are in the right age group, too. Don't have teenagers in the group when you are evaluating denture cream.

Size of group: From eight to ten is the right size. Too much bigger gets unwieldy and loses the intimacy that leads to the exchange of ideas you seek. Fewer won't tell you enough.

How to proceed: Assemble the group in a proper-sized room—not a gigantic hall that makes everyone feel uncomfortable and uneasy. The keynote must be ease and informality. Serve them coffee to foster relaxation. Then start with a little talk thanking them for coming and stating how you value their judgments and are eager to have their opinions.

Make it plain that there are no wrong or right answers—all you want are opinions and reactions.

Tape It—it's vital that you make a tape recording of the procedure. It is impossible for a moderator to lead a group and take notes at the same time; this not only breaks concentration, but throws participants off from time to time. For instance, if you were in a focus group and made a comment that the moderator quickly put in his notes, you might be either proud or put off, which would affect your future contributions. And if you stated an opinion that he did not bother to note down, you might be peeved that he didn't deem it as important as your neighbor's comments, which he did record.

Taping allows you to review the results and evaluate them in the quiet of your office. It permits you to pick up subtleties you may have missed during the session. It also proves to other members of your organization that these statements did occur and were not merely your biased interpretations of the facts as you chose to hear them—always a danger.

Of course, in this post-Watergate era, you never tape a session without informing the participants. Do it casually, because people tend to be somewhat unnerved by cameras and tape recorders. The knowledge that they are being recorded for posterity frequently causes them to act unnaturally. I had a client who was a real cranky curmudgeon. Meetings used to be unpleasant and minimally productive until one day I brought in a tape recorder to be sure, as I told him, I didn't miss any of the pearls that kept pouring forth from his creative lips. You never saw such a transformation. He buttoned his jacket and began to orate as though he were giving the Gettysburg Address. The awareness that his words were being preserved for posterity changed his demeanor, and from that point on meetings were a pleasure.

But that's not the sort of reaction you want from focus group participants. What you want is instinctual responses and no self-consciousness. They will become used to the tape recorder after a while and will totally forget its presence.

The Questions—Questions must be prepared carefully so that they are psychologically structured to suggest nothing, but merely to elicit reaction. If you ask a straight "yes" or "no" question, you can kill the entire proceedings.

For instance, I was doing a focus group for an architectural-style lamp that the manufacturer wished to bring out in a less-tech consumer version. If I showed the lamp and then asked, "Do you like it?", I risked getting a "no" answer, in which case I'd have had to fold up my tent and go home. Instead, I asked, "In which room would you use this lamp?" This power-of-suggestion query moved the participants past the position of making a decision as to whether or not they like the lamp, and into the realm of deciding how and where it would be used in their homes. That sort of question evokes ideas, and one woman's ideas spark another's. "I'd put it in my teenager's room next to the chair he studies in. Right now, I bought this expensive lamp that works fine at first, when he's sitting up straight. But in ten minutes, he's slouched down, and in fifteen minutes he's lying on the floor with his feet on the chair. This lamp would move with him instead of him having to move to the light." It was a great line, too, and we used it in our advertising. That's the sort of material that comes out of focus groups. Her suggestion got a lot of head-nodding around the room, and prompted another woman to say: "That would be good for my husband's workbench, too. He can't see so well anymore and his lamp is in the middle of the table. When he works on little things at the ends of the bench, he could just swing the lamp right over it."

The suggestions kept flying, with every participant wanting to outdo the other with ideas of how her family would use this great lamp. We got a wealth of in-use suggestions and a definitely positive reaction.

Now that you know the product is acceptable and you have a pretty good idea of where it would be used, we come to the next major question: How much are they willing to pay for it?

The Price of a new product is a vital factor, not only in the effect it has on sales, but the total effect on your profits. Too often in small businesses, new product prices are determined solely upon costs. "We pay so much for materials, labor, packaging, overhead, sales commission, thus the price must be $10." But you are operating in a vacuum. How do you know people will pay $10 for it? And, more importantly, how do you know that they won't just as readily pay $15 for it? The classic error made by small business is to underprice rather than overprice.

We asked the focus group participants how much they expected to pay for our lamp. Of course, that's not how the query was worded, because that would be too loose and broad a question. Instead we gave them price categories and asked which one was correct. And were we surprised— happily. The lamp had been slated for a $19.95 price tag. The conclusion from the group was that $25 would be the ideal price.

Don't forget that price is a major element in creating consumer opinion. A higher price conveys better quality instantly, and if it is for a gift, makes both giver and recipient feel better about the whole transaction. Have you ever noticed that at Christmastime, the department stores set up tables of gifts arranged according to price? Ten-dollar gifts on this table, $20 gifts on that one. Watch how shoppers proceed with their lists. "Let's see, Aunt Sophie gave us a $10 gift last year—so that's what I'll buy for her." And so on. Notice that no one is spending too much time evaluating whether or not the gift is *worth* $10. Who can tell these days?

The main thing is that everyone's comfortable. The giver is spending the correct amount, and the recipient knows that the donor has behaved properly.

Checking with a focus group about the price of your product can pay handsome dividends.

The Moderator—It could be you, of course. But not if the group participants know you and your affiliation with the product. It is imperative that the moderator be impartial in the eyes of the group. Otherwise their reactions will be colored by their personal methods of dealing with your feelings.

There are some people who dearly love to see others squirm. If they know it's your product, your store, your company, they'll get great pleasure in pointing out what a useless piece of junk you've produced. Then there are the Mr. Nice Guys who cannot bear to make anyone unhappy. They'll bend over backwards to be flattering. Neither of these reactions helps your cause. So it's best to be totally anonymous.

You can hire a moderator; there are many professional firms that handle focus groups and charge up to a few thousand dollars, or you can save money by going to your local university's MBA Program office. Ask for the dean, and suggest the focus group as part of a market research class project.

The Participants—Where to Find Them—In this era of bigness, people like to feel they can provide some input and have an effect on what and how things are offered in the marketplace. You will be surprised how pleased people are that you care for and want their opinions; who doesn't feel flattered by such interest? Go to local church or synagogue groups and ask them to send participants (be sure to give an accurate profile of the age, income and other demographic features you require) and then offer a contribution to the institution. Some focus groups give gifts or money to the participants. I have never found the need for that, nor have I ever seen that the offer affected attendance. They either want to come because it's an enjoyable prospect, or not, but the promise of remuneration has never seemed important. However, if you want to distribute token "thank you" gifts, it can't hurt.

Why You Should Use Focus Groups—Every business needs a focus group periodically. Not only before you introduce a new product, but also to find out what the market thinks about your existing ones. It is an excellent idea to get opinions from customers and prospects on their perception of your company. Do they think of you as a buying source only for a specific group of merchandise that represents a fraction of your line? You know how you have favorite restaurants? One is your steak place, one establishment is where you go for fish, and perhaps you have another preferred spaghetti spot. Yet, chances are, if you examined their menus, you'd find that each one offers all the foods mentioned above. You have evolved your own perceptions of their areas of specialization, and that's that. Do you see how this same sort of mind-set can be affecting *your* business? If you had a needlepoint shop, a focus group among customers and prospects might well reveal that most people come to you only for special yarns and complicated cross-stitch projects and are totally unaware that you sell kits and other lower-priced merchandise for which they are now going to K-Mart. If you are a computer supplier, you may learn that the market sees you as a source only for hardware and custom software and has no idea that you sell software packages.

If you do not correct these misconceptions, you will be missing out on a substantial piece of business. But how could you know of the existence of these erroneous perceptions—unless you uncovered them at a focus group?

An owner of a chain of low-priced women's shoe stores in Milwaukee decided to expand into high-priced shoes. He had the locations; he had the stores. Why not just put in an expensive shoe department in each one? He invested a small fortune in redesigning the stores and creating a fancy shoe corner in each one, and they died, of course. If he had checked out the potential via focus groups, he would have learned that a woman who wishes to buy a $100 pair of leather shoes does not care to rub elbows with customers who are frantically fighting their way through piles of vinyl boots and plastic wedgies. She wants to be pampered in a quiet elegant ambience, and to walk out with a bag that bears the snob stamp of a fancy shop. And he would have learned that a sortie into the rarified levels of $100-and-upward footwear required a new chain of locations.

Making move-ahead business decisions always requires guts and risk. But if you have a device that can provide indications of the pitfalls and possibilities to be anticipated, why not minimize your risk? Before embarking upon your next major expansion project, check it out first with a focus group. It's a small investment that can ultimately save you thousands of dollars.

THE BUDGET 3

Where to spend it

The word "budget" usually connotes caution with cash and limited income. But in my experience "advertising budgets" exist strictly in the province of big-money land. The little fellow's advertising expenditures are usually handled in a freewheeling way that would horrify the structured scientific soul of a Harvard Business School type. In the impulsive play-it-by-ear world of small business the "advertising budget" is just a series of figures compiled at the beginning of each year to make everyone feel that correct modern business methods are being observed.

"Work up a recommended advertising program for the year," the ad agency is told. After much research, selective readership statistics, and arithmetic, the agency comes up with a conscientious schedule of where and how the money should be allocated. It is impressively typed in triplicate and then distributed at a meeting consisting of the agency and all important, interested client personnel. There, amid a great deal of heated discussion of the budget, followed by judicious evaluation and cautious consolidation (translation: nit-picking and hacking away), the annual advertising program is set. And everyone exits in a flurry of good fellowship and the satisfaction of a job well done.

Then the next day the principal competitor comes out with a knock-off of the company's chief product, and the whole program is obliterated, as the company president hollers for immediate ads and direct-mail promotions to counteract this gross indignity.

In small business nothing is permanent and irrevocable. You have to meet special situations as they arise. It is this ability to be flexible that gives the smaller business a big advantage over big business. You can work fast and hit fast without being forced to await decisions and approvals from above.

Still, you should arrive at a budget—some idea of how much the company can spend on advertising for the coming year and where you think it should go. Even though you all know that it can be altered, it's a framework to work with and gives a certain amount of direction to the total promotional effort.

The question I am asked most frequently at seminars is: "How much should we spend for advertising a year?" The answer is written on the wind. Well, not quite that elusive. The usual figure is one percent of the annual gross. I say "usual" because this figure changes radically from industry to industry. Designer-jeans companies spend between 40 and 50 percent of their gross, according to the *New York Times*. Cosmetics companies who are selling names rather than products, spend at least 20 percent. So the figure of one percent is merely an average.

I have had students whose stores grossed $30,000 a year. If they used the one-percent guideline, they would allot $300 as their annual advertising budget, thereby ensuring that sales would never move above that figure. You must use your judgment. If it's a start-up situation, a bigger advertising investment is required initially. Whatever you feel you can realistically afford is it. Just arrive at a figure at the beginning of the year and try to stick closely to it.

Your next step is to break down the budget into proper areas of expenditure: media, direct mail, catalogs, trade shows, and public relations . . . which leads to selecting and using all these elements wisely and economically.

MEDIA SELECTION 4

Putting your money where the markets are

The Value of Trade Publications

Every business has its trade publications. They are the life force of an industry. Every individual who is in any way involved in that industry reads the trade publications, since they are the prime sources of news and educational information that he must have to function efficiently. If you want to know what everyone is doing and where and how, it's in the trade publication. If you want others to know what you are doing, you must advertise in the trade publication. There are many ways and reasons to use trade advertising.

Institutional Advertising

I hate to mention "institutional" because the word is usually an anathema to pragmatic, hard-nosed businessmen.

Institutional advertising is the sort of ad that says: "Hello, everybody, here we are. This is our name, and this is what we do." It doesn't really sell anything other than image. To the small businessman this is a luxury he usually feels he cannot afford. He likes to see every buck spent produce a tangible result—like a sales lead or a sale. Institutional ads don't produce inquiries. They don't produce immediate sales, but they are necessary to achieve some very important effects and to solve some very serious problems.

Take a client of mine who suddenly enjoyed tremendous growth. Since production facilities had not yet caught up with the new sales figures, they were behind in deliveries and behind in correspondence. While they were working feverishly on expansion plans to accommodate this new activity, the competition took advantage of their chaos to whisper around that the company was bordering on bankruptcy. When these rumors started to become dangerous, it was important to run institutional advertising to let the industry know that they were still in business. A series of ads appeared in all the trade publications that made it quite apparent that the company was very much alive and kicking. However, it was almost too late, and the company had been put on the defensive.

Prestige Buildup

"Prestige"—that elusive word that contributes so concretely to growth. The subliminal effect of seeing a name repeatedly has the effect of attaching the name to that class of product.

Of course, it took millions to develop the association of the name "Kleenex" with tissues and "Frigidaire" with refrigerators, but on a smaller scale that sort of status is what can be achieved by consistent advertising in the trade media.

Buying-Time Reminders

Direct mail acts immediately or not at all. It directs the recipient to take a specific action *now* and then toss the piece away. It's not meant to leave a lasting impression; direct mail is a one-shot deal. But ads are there, in front of the buyers for a day, a week, a month. And every time they go through the publication, your ad registers and builds up a subconscious reminder factor that clicks into action when ordering time comes around.

Opening Doors for Salesmen

It's bad enough when your salesman walks into a new prospect and says, "Hello, I'm Charlie Rollins," and the buyer says, "Charlie who?"

But it's worse when the salesman comes back with, "You know, Charlie

Rollins, from Tooth and Nail Medical Supply Company," and the prospect says, "The Tooth and What Company?"

Then your man is in trouble, and it's your fault.

Trade advertising makes the company name instantly familiar to prospects and opens doors for salesmen. It assures a warmer reception on cold calls, when they need all the help they can get, and it keeps the doors open and makes their jobs easier.

I've heard small businessmen say proudly, "We don't need trade advertising. Everyone in the business knows us." Sure—maybe last year, last month, or last week, but new buyers come into the field every day; new businesses open every week. If you don't keep your name around constantly, where everyone can see it, it will be as quickly forgotten as last year's Miss America.

Introducing a New Product

When you are bringing out a new product or launching a special promotion, trade advertising must be the hub of it. Your big announcement should hit the pages of the trade publication and be coordinated with all other elements of the promotion.

Preparing a Reception for Your Direct Mail

You would hesitate to buy a television set from a street peddler. Who knows what's inside the cabinet, and where do you go for service? So how can you expect anyone to buy your products from a cold direct-mail solicitation if they don't know who you are?

A mailing comes out of nowhere. It's an impersonal piece of paper that is dropped on a desk by a usually faceless postman. It has no connection to a real, live company—unless you build one. Trade-paper advertising builds your image as a substantial, reliable, known quantity. They know your name; they know you are a solid organization and not some hole-in-the-wall operation. When your mailing hits their desks, they recognize, read, and respond. Trade advertising establishes your position, and thus increases the effectiveness of your direct mail.

WHICH TRADE PUBLICATIONS TO PICK

First, see if you can get your hands on a *Standard Rate & Data, Business Publications* issue (the green volume) and also the *Consumer Magazine* issue (the orange volume). These are the bibles of the media buyer. They list all publications according to industry or category and give rates, circulation, and every kind of information you need. You must be a subscriber to get copies, and every advertising agency is. Ask a neighborhood ad agency to give you back copies. They are issued every few months, and the oldies only get thrown out anyway. Or you can find them at your local library's reference room.

Now call or write each magazine in your industry and ask (1) for copies of their three latest issues, and (2) to have a space salesman call. Before you see the salesman, carefully read and analyze each magazine yourself.

Design and appearance: Does it look well printed, well designed? Now don't say, "What do I know? I'm not an art critic." There's a great deal you can tell by instinct. You may not be able to define your reaction, but you can rely here on that old bromide, "I don't know anything about art; I just know what I like." A poorly printed publication—and I've seen some lulus that looked as if they'd been run off on a hand press for distribution at smoker movies—will have smeared, grey-looking type, fuzzy pictures, and cheap paper. If it's poorly designed (maybe too few pictures, too heavy concentration of type), it will not invite readership. If it looks cheap and shoddy, it will make your company look cheap and shoddy, so skip it.

How much advertising does it carry? This is a good clue to a publication's effectiveness as a selling medium. If it carries just a desultory scattering of ads, then it is wanting in some department, because if it were a valuable publication that reached and affected buyers, the ad agency media people would have put their client's money into it. If they bypassed it, so should you.

Of course, that's not a hard and fast rule. When a magazine is new, it might not yet have picked up advertising momentum but still have a very high rate of readership. Be sure you look through a few issues so that you are not misled by seasonal slumps. Summer issues carry a relatively light advertising load.

Whose advertising does it carry? Notice the quality of the ads and the companies represented. If the magazine seems filled with poorly put-together ads (of companies you never even heard of), they are probably pub-set. That means the publication's usually minimal art facility has produced the ad free for a company which could not afford ad agency services. At the risk of sounding like a snob, if it doesn't attract better advertisers than that, it isn't much of a publication.

Does the publication appeal to your specific segment of the market? Most fields have many facets, and each trade magazine develops its own sort of constituency. You want to be sure that you're going in the magazine that reaches your part of the market. For example, in the interior design field there are two market categories—traditional and contemporary, and there are two major publications in the field. If you look through the magazines, you will notice that the editorial content and merchandise advertised in one is heavily traditional, with a token contemporary section. The other magazine is filled almost exclusively with contemporary furnishings. In the stationery field there are social stationers and commercial stationers. One magazine is basically commercial, with a section devoted to greeting cards and sundry social-stationery merchandise, another publication is weighted the other way around.

You select the publication that is slanted predominantly towards your specific area. If it has merely a section devoted to your interest, that means it reaches just a section of the market. Why pay full price for an ad that reaches only a fraction of your market?

HOW TO LISTEN TO SPACE SALESMEN

These eager gentlemen, the space salesmen, are some of the best-trained, best-informed, and best-equipped salespeople you will ever encounter. They will present you with enough charts, graphs, readership studies, and attaché case loads of facts and figures to make the mind boggle.

Listen to them and then ask your questions.

Watch out for alibi words that indicate poor circulation, like "secondary pass-along circulation." That means they are trying to claim that their publication is read not only by a subscriber, but is passed on to the crowd of ardent fans who are milling around his desk just awaiting their turn at the magazine. Since this readership claim cannot be measured, if it indeed exists, forget it. It is usually the weak statement of a weak publication.

I've heard all kinds of circulation allegations by some overzealous, underequipped space salesman. Like the fellow who told me that his magazine had the "highest restroom circulation" in the industry. You realize, of course, that you would then be enjoying a sort of captive readership, a unique situation that assures intensive perusal of the publication. To my knowledge, no statistical organization has yet chosen to compile and evaluate these alleged facts and figures. You know that any space salesman touting this sort of data has to have a poor magazine. All you want to know about is proven, audited circulation.

DIRECT RESPONSE—THE HOT NEW MEDIUM

"Direct response" is a whole new concept that has arisen in the last few years. It had existed previously in a few fields but has proliferated to the point that the category now has its own special section in *Standard Rate & Data*—an accolade of advertising trade recognition tantamount to being invited to join the United Nations.

In effect, direct response is actually a hybrid: a cross between direct mail and a trade publication. It is a collection of product postcards, bound together in booklet form. Each advertiser has a single card, arranged in standard format, with the product on the front and a return address on back. The interested reader merely detaches the card and mails it in. It's easy and immediate.

This medium works very much like direct mail, with a few differences—some good, some bad. On the plus side you get mailed to a huge interested list without paying the mammoth postage and handling costs all by yourself. You travel with a good crowd. The collection of cards has the substantial effect of a buying source guide and is likely to be held on to far longer than would a single piece of direct mail. On the negative side you can show only one product or service on a card and are restricted to a very limiting format.

The direct-response medium can pull a tremendous volume of inquiries. Many of my students have reported success stories that resulted not only in large numbers of inquiries, but in a high percentage of sales conversions.

If you are looking for inquiries, if you have a sales organization that is dependent on your referrals, this is a sure way to get them.

WHERE TO PUT YOUR MONEY

In the final analysis, which trade publication do you put your money on? After you have heard all the pitches and analyzed all the publications, it's often still hard to decide where to go.

If your budget can stand it, go in all of them—that is, all the publications that reach your market and are reliable books. There are usually at least two of the category in each field. I suggest that you hit all of them because the trade publications are important. Their goodwill is a handy thing to have, and you can get help from them that is available nowhere else. When you need special trade information, seek new distributors or salespeople; they will supply you with the facts. When you have new products to launch or new promotions to announce, they will give you free publicity in their pages.

MEDIA SELECTION

That's why it is better to divide your budget—to go less frequently in each so that you can cover them all. However, if your budget is such that you will be spreading your ads too thin—like two times here, two times there—then settle on one magazine. Fewer than three insertions are a waste. The frequency figure that produces the best results is six.

WHAT SIZE AD?

Full pages are lovely but not necessary as a steady diet. The best method is to launch with a full-page ad—start out the year with a splash—and then go to island-half sizes, and maybe throw in another full page later on.

The island-half is a pet size of mine. It's bigger and costs more than a half and is smaller and costs less than two-thirds. The advantage of this unique unit is that its shape makes it almost impossible to have another ad on the page. You dominate in a solo spot, happily surrounded by editorial matter.

Another striking and economical technique is to use two vertical halves on facing pages (or one-third and two-thirds) with no other ads on the spread. Of course, you have to request this setup. And although you would be taxed an additional charge for such premium positioning in a consumer publication, trade magazines are more cooperative and generally impose no extra tariff. It's a great way to command a double-page spread for the price of a single page.

Now, here's the budget bonus in this split-page method. If you were to run full pages in six issues, you would be billed at a six-time rate. However, two facing halves in six issues count as 12 insertions, and you would earn the lower 12-time rate!

Sometimes you may have to go to quarter pages. Okay, if you must, you must, although most publications stack up one-quarter-page ad atop another, and you never know where your ad begins and the one in the upper bunk leaves off—but at least the size is adequate to use readable-sized type and show a decent-sized picture.

But I'd say to skip one-sixth and one-eighth pages in trade magazines. Those small units get buried in the back and always convey a little, unprepossessing impression. Why spend money to let everyone know that you can't afford to spend more?

POSITION IS EVERYTHING

"Hey, I got us a terrific position in the publication—right-hand page in the beginning of the book!" How many times has an ad agency phoned those words triumphantly to clients as though some marvellous readership ensurance has been achieved?

It's a myth. Never has it been proved that a right-hand outpulls a left-hand page, or that ads on page three do better than those on page 63. Yet all ad agency insertion orders inevitably read "Right-hand page requested, as far front as possible." It's just one of those things that makes the agency feel they have done something special for the client and makes the client feel his agency is really on the ball.

As for the benefits of an ad appearing in the front of the magazine—do you always read a magazine from front to back, or are you like me and millions of others who open in the middle, maybe flip through to find items of interest, or perhaps go right to a favorite feature?

The Well-Read Location—Check through the publication to find favorite features, well-read columnists and other spots that draw readers. In a trade magazine, everyone turns to the New Products section, or the Trade Notes section that tells about job changes and obits. Ask for your ad to appear in those positions.

Be creative in your position-choosing process. A woman's clothing store ran a Mother's Day ad in the Sports Section of the daily newspaper pages that received heavy male readership. The ad read, "We know what she wants for Mother's Day." It played upon the helplessness most men seem to feel about gift selections for their wives and mothers, and offered the guidance and assurance of gift-giving success that they all seek. The ad was tremendously successful.

The Power of Persuasion—I have evolved a very effective method for getting good positions in publications. It's called "Hollering." I demand of the space salesman to give us the position we covet. I impose threats of taking our ads elsewhere. I nag. It may not make me the most popular person down at the publications, but it gets action.

A rug importer whose account we handled wanted to advertise in HFD, a newspaper-style tabloid trade publication. But he longed for the front page which had carried a strip-across-the-bottom-ad by the same advertiser for as many years as I've seen the publication. This company had placed a "till forbid" order which ran in perpetuity for that prime spot, and my client could not have it. So he pouted and refused to go in. I kept after the space salesman to get us on the front page, someway or other. One morning, he phoned in a high state of excitement to advise that he had just come from a meeting where they announced the one-time availability of a tip-on ad on the front page of the issue that would be distributed at the major market show in Chicago. "How much?" I asked.

"Fifteen hundred dollars. plus you provide us with the printed pieces that we'll glue onto the upper left-hand corner of the front page." "We'll take it!" I said and then called my client, who was ambivalent. "That's a lot of money for one insertion, plus the cost of printing those thousands of pieces." I convinced him that it was a once-in-a-lifetime opportunity that we must take, and he agreed. We printed a 4-in. × 6-in. piece in purple ink, showing the picture of a rug under his name, in huge letters. He phoned us from Chicago the day the show opened, so ecstatic that he was almost babbling. Since the exhibit was held at the Hilton, the publication knew that most of the hotel rooms were occupied by people attending the show, and had placed copies of the paper in front of every door. As our client walked down the hotel corridors, he saw his name staring up at him from every room. Instant immortality! Needless to say, we bought that spot forever and contracted to take it whenever it was available. That came from "hollering." It's a technique I recommend, but use it judiciously, not obnoxiously.

You have seen the ad at least four times before it hits print. Then you check it again in proof form. By the time it's out, you and everyone at the office are sick of it. After it appears once, the tendency is to say: "Not that ad again! Let's have something new." But that's wrong.

Actually the ad hasn't even started to reach all the customers, let alone saturate the market. Your personal overexposure is causing you to commit the common sin of public underexposure. A print ad should appear and appear and reappear, over and over again.

Do you notice how frequently a single TV commercial is repeated? And do you also notice how your kids can soon recite some TV spots verbatim? That hammering-away repeater technique is motivated by marketing know how, not frugality. They don't change the commercial after a few showings.

They keep pounding away until you're sick of it. At that point they know the message has sunk in.

Print advertising works the same way. The constant repetition is vital to get your message to saturate the market and become planted firmly in the buyers' minds. As a rule of thumb, when you are just about sick of an ad, it's just about reaching the customer. So let it run, let it run, let it run. Look at the money you save in ad-preparation costs!

REMEMBER THE REGIONALS

If there are regional magazines in your industry, give them a break. The South and West seem partial to this sort of homespun gazetteering.

Though these regionally made magazines merely duplicate the circulation you are reaching in the national publications, they command a local loyalty you cannot ignore. Besides, their rates are moderate. If you should open a branch there or have any newsworthy action in the vicinity, they'll be on the spot with photographers and reporters and give you publicity treatment worthy of the opening of a Hollywood delicatessen.

TIMING: WHEN TO ADVERTISE

If your big buying season is in the spring, you would naturally schedule your ads during the spring months. Hit them when they're ready to buy—that's the rule.

If you are a manufacturer or distributor, there are other considerations as well. There are the big trade shows, and those special pre-show issues, trade-show issues, and post-show issues. According to the space salespeople, you've "gotta" be in all three, which blows the total annual budget for some of us, and leaves three-quarters of the year with no exposure whatever. Ridiculous. I opt for the show issue—the one that's mailed out before the show and distributed lavishly at the show, which makes it a real bargain all around. Magazine ad rates are predicated upon circulation—the more readers, the more they charge per page. Makes sense. That means you are buying an ad based on a specific promised circulation, but the magazines distribute thousands of extra copies at the shows, which is, in effect, bonus circulation for which you are not charged. In other words, it's free. Plus the fact that everyone reads that issue, whether they intend to attend or not. Not only do you get high visibility, but important visibility. This is one situation where your absence can be apparent. If everyone of importance is in this major issue and you are not, the inferences that may be drawn are that (1) you are not an important company, and/or (2) you are in some sort of trouble.

Also remember that those copies distributed at shows get heavy readership. I don't know about you, but when I attend a show, either as an exhibitor or a buyer, I am beat at the end of the day and tend to flop into a chair or bed and watch television and read every piece of literature that's in the room.

CONSUMER MAGAZINE ADVERTISING— THE BIG TIME

Wouldn't you love to see your wares displayed in *Time, Newsweek, Better Homes & Gardens, House Beautiful,* and the like? It's so impressive, so glamorous. Just so you have some idea how big the big time can be, consider the tariffs these publications exact for the privilege of appearing in their pages. Here are the going rates for single page, black-and-white ads:

Time—$60,525
Newsweek—$44,040
Sports Illustrated—$38,585
Better Homes & Gardens—$65,300

So the next time you flip casually through one of these publications, move slowly. At these prices each ad deserves at least a lingering glance.

If you are a manufacturer or distributor, the purpose of consumer magazine advertising is to create acceptance and demand at the critical spot—the point of purchase. In other words, its purpose is to entice the populace into stores to ask for your product or at least to recognize and be persuaded to select it from all others. If you are a retailer, you probably confine your advertising to local newspapers, radio, and television. The purpose of consumer magazine advertising would be to create a prestige impression and image for your establishment as well as to promote sales of specific merchandise.

"Why are you saying this if rates are so prohibitive?" you may be wondering. That is a reasonable question for anyone with a small budget. For many readers a single black-and-white page in *Time* would cost two years' projected outlay for advertising.

There is a way. It's called MNI (Media Networks, Inc.). You can buy one page in *Time, Newsweek, Sports Illustrated, U.S. News & World Report* for a total of as little as $3,815. That's for four ads, one in each of these publications!

Sounds fantastic, but it's a fact. However, your ad will only appear in those issues being distributed to a specific regional area. For instance, the price of $3,815 buys you exposure in Pittsburgh. If you want to reach other cities, they are available at prices varying according to the circulation.

If you wanted to reach women, you ad could appear in *Better Homes & Gardens, House Beautiful,* and *Metropolitan Home*—all for just $3,685, but just to the specific market area you order.

The way it works is MNI publishes full-page sections of advertising for each of the almost 100 market areas they cover. These preprinted units are bound into the subscription (not newsstand) copies of participating publications going to specific Zip Code areas. Your ad appears in these fancy national magazines right next to the Coca-Cola and IBM ads. The consumer who sees your ad has no idea that it appears only in his area and not in the copies being read in another locality; is he ever impressed!

I know, because that was me. I picked up my copy of *Newsweek* one day and was flabbergasted to see an ad by my local liquor store. Now I know that liquor cannot be sold over state lines, so what was he doing in a national magazine? I thought he was just a marginal hole-in-the-wall operation, and here he was blowing a bundle on a single ad. Then I noticed a series of small code letters at the bottom of the page: "WES 3." I live in the county of Westchester, and it was March (the third month), so this was apparently some sort of key number. I phoned *Newsweek*'s ad department and was told to call MNI, from whom I got the facts.

We had a Westchester client, with two high-quality menswear shops, who had been advertising in local papers with minimal results. We placed his ad in the MNI Suburban Network (*Newsweek, Sports Illustrated, Time,* and *U.S. News & World Report*) for Westchester County at a cost that was less than he was spending for a month of local newspaper advertising. The results were astounding.

Customers streamed into his stores absolutely awed. "Gee, George," they said admiringly. "I thought you were just a little local operation. I guess you must be a lot bigger if you can afford to advertise in *Newsweek.*" People think if you're rich you must be smart and successful, and their whole image of you alters into one of total confidence. Besides this instant benefit, you derive an invaluable long-term value from these ads in the form of merchandising tie-ins.

Many years ago when *Life* magazine was the number one in the nation, advertisers used to spend thousands of dollars to insert one-inch ads in the back of the publication that featured a batch of jammed together words in six-point "optician" type. When I asked the space salesman why would anyone spend so much money on ads that were destined to be unread, he responded, "For the merchandising tie-in benefit. Once your ad appears in *Life,* all your ads and literature can forever after feature the famous red-and-white rectangle with the words, "As Advertised in *Life.*"

Thus when you run in MNI, you can get mounted counter-card reprints of your ad carrying the words, "AS ADVERTISED IN TIME," or *Newsweek,* or *Better Homes & Gardens.* Featured on store counters and windows, they carry clout that impresses customers, and all your literature can bear this effective message forever!

If you are a retailer in an area that is covered by MNI, it's the way to go. If you are a national distributor, you can use MNI to target specific markets. Remember what was uncovered in the "Interrogating the Boss" section. If you discovered that your heaviest concentration of sales and sales potential are in specific geographic areas, then MNI advertising is an efficient, economical method of reaching exactly these buyers.

There's yet another way to use the big-time consumer publications economically. That's by using geographic and demographic editions. Most of the major magazines offer this kind of select media buying. *The Wall Street Journal* offers four American editions—Eastern, Midwest, Southwest, and Pacific. If you are attempting to test a new mail order item, the Southwest edition is an excellent low-cost way to evaluate the potential of the product.

TV Guide has an almost endless variation of geographic editions enabling you to reach specific areas. If your product, service or establishment lends itself to the *TV Guide* audience, you will find this a highly effective medium.

Demographic editions allow you to place an ad based on how your audience lives. The breakdowns are according to profession or income. *Time* enables you to reach doctors, for instance. *Reader's Digest* demos according to income. If you are a new company that has just gone public and would like to catch the eyes of some Wall Street wonder boy who might latch on to your stock and zoom it, you might consider running an ad in the Eastern edition of *The Wall Street Journal*.

All this information on rates and editions appears in the *Standard Rate & Data, Consumer Magazines* issue (orange volume). To locate MNI, look up Media Networks, Inc. in your local phone book for a regional branch. (They are in most major cities.) Or write or phone them in New York City, which is their home office.

Amortizing a Consumer Ad

You can get tremendous mileage out of a single consumer ad if you play your collateral material right. A large ad in the right publication can be merchandised to the hilt and used to any number of advantages—for example, as the basis of a campaign to buy admission to a new market.

We had a client who imported cookware and longed to proselytize among that group of rich, ripe consumers—brides.

Until you get involved with the bridal market, you have no real concept of the kind of wild spending that goes on there. When you realize that many brides are ready and willing to buy a lifetime's worth of furnishings within a few short months, you get some idea of what kind of sales potential exists for manufacturers of housewares.

It isn't just what the brides buy themselves. Today, wedding-gift giving has been honed into an efficient system that eliminates any possibility of poor choices (and all elements of sentiment). It's called the Bridal Registry. This procedure has the bride-to-be "registering" her gift preferences in the shop of her choice. Months before the wedding, she calls upon the store's bridal registry department; there she is greeted like visiting royalty and taken on a personal guided tour of the various departments to select her preferences in every facet of furnishings, from china to cheeseboards. The accompanying bridal representative carefully chronicles the choices on a printed registry form, and the wedding guests-to-be are notified that "the bride is registered at ------ store." This enables them to phone the store and say, "What does she want that costs $50 that nobody else has bought yet?"

As you can see, it's all heart . . . and big business.

The aim of our client, as of every household-equipment manufacturer, was to get his brand name specified on the bride's registry form. After all, she's the purchasing agent, and her specification means sure sales.

How to get to the bride was easy: There are two magazines that are read avidly by young women who have set the date (and that are also read by their mothers; this is one pass-along circulation that's valid). The real problem was how to get to the bridal registry service representatives and to the store buyers.

One ad did the job. We used four-color because the outstanding asset of the cookware was its vibrant colors: to use black-and-white would have saved money but lost the campaign. At the bottom of the ad was the fiendishly clever hook:

FREE GIFT FOR YOU

Fill in and mail this coupon now, and we'll send a valuable "whatever-you-wish dish" to your Bridal Registry store IN YOUR NAME.
Pick it up whenever you wish.
Name _____
Address _____
My Store _____

The strategy was this:

1. The store bridal consultant would be put in the pleasant position of presenting her bridal customer with a gift, which cost the store nothing (and in so doing, would become aware of the line of cookware).

2. The bride-to-be would be introduced to the advantages of the cookware and possibly induced to specify it in her registry listing.

3. The manufacturer would have an opening wedge to the formerly closed doors of the store cookware buyers.

Before the ad appeared, we made sure to avail ourselves of every facility offered by the magazine's merchandising department. And that is a bargain benefit not to be overlooked. Every good consumer publication has a department devoted to producing material and services to promote the products advertised in its pages—materials such as reprints, preprints, mailings, listings in newsletters, presentations to store buyers. Their cooperation is boundless. Thus we were able to obtain full-color preprints of the ad and mounted counter cards at unbelievably low prices. The material was distributed by the company salesman and also mailed to bridal registry departments throughout the country.

The promotion was a huge success. The ad pulled one of the highest reader responses ever recorded by the magazine. (It happened to be a great ad.) Gift dish packages, including brochures of the full line of cookware, were sent to thousands of young women via their bridal registries. As a result, the manufacturer gained entry into the bridal registry of nearly every major department store in the country.

Merchandise Your Ads

Don't just let your ads sit there in the pages of magazines; move them out. Make reprints of every ad you run, bearing the words "As advertised in...." with the names of every publication on your advertising schedule. That goes for trade magazine advertising as well.

After all, you send out a pile of mail every day: bills, statements, correspondence. Why allow the envelopes to go out half-empty? Pack them with promotional literature. Include ad reprints to give additional exposure to your advertising.

COOPERATIVE ADVERTISING

It's always nice to have someone else share expenses. It allows you to spread your budget so much farther.

If you sell a product or service to dealers, cooperative advertising is of great benefit to you. If you are the dealer who resells the product or service, cooperative advertising is of great benefit to you. This is one arrangement where everybody wins.

The procedure is just what the name implies. The dealer runs ads, usually in his local media, for which the manufacturer picks up part of the tab. The manufacturer loves it because the ads promote his products in more media than he could otherwise afford. And the dealer loves it because it enables him to afford to run ads that promote his name and bring in business.

If you are the manufacturer, encourage your dealers to take advantage of your cooperative-advertising program. Offer to pay 15 percent, 25 percent, or 50 percent—whatever you feel you can afford—of the cost of the space or time purchased by the dealer to promote your products. Payment is made, either in cash or in merchandise credit, upon submission of bills and tear sheets from the media.

To make it easier for the dealer, and to ensure that your product is shown and described as you would like, offer prepared artwork and newspaper slicks. These are finished, screened pieces of art that are ready for use by local newspapers who merely slug in the retailer's name, logo, and selling price. If you leave the art preparation to the retailer, he will either never get around to getting it done, or will relegate the creative job to the publication's art department. Ugh. If you supply prepared material, you ensure that ads appearing for your products all over the country bear a cohesive look, to convey the effect of a national campaign.

If you are a retailer, ask all your suppliers for cooperative help in the form of payments, credits, advertising material, display material.

It sounds like the manufacturer gives and the retailer gets. But there are ways for the manufacturer also to get co-op funding for his own advertising.

When I was ad manager for a manufacturer of transparent acetate products, I was stunned to come upon a two-page color spread in *Time*, featuring our principal competitor. They were the same size as we (small)—so where did they suddenly come up with the funding for such a major outlay? Then I spotted the small orange rectangle at the lower right-hand corner: "Kodak." At that time, both companies purchased all their acetate from Eastman Kodak and the Celanese Corporation. I had a suspicion about the source of the financing, but was not certain. I have found that the best way to get information fast is to use shock tactics. So I phoned our Kodak salesman, who knew I had buying influence (and knew that we were major purchasers) and said flatly: "Tom, as of tomorrow, we are giving all our business to Celanese." After he stopped stammering in shock I told him that I was angered at the ad they had done for our competitor. It was a feint, but it worked. He said quickly, "I'll phone you back in a few minutes," and did he ever. "We'll send representatives from our ad agency over tomorrow and they'll prepare a two-page spread in *Time* for you, in full color. We'll do the photography, color separations, typography, everything. And pay for the space, too, of course." And the next day, three fellows from J. Walter Thompson came in (they always come in threes) and worked out all the details.

After that, I phoned every supplier we had: steel manufacturer for the ring-binder parts we used, paper mills for the binder covers, and others. And I picked up thousands of dollars in co-op money for our advertising. Go through your production operation and check out all your sources of supplies and phone them to request co-op funding. Alcoa, Reynolds, US Steel, DuPont—most major corporations offer these benefits. According to Federal law, they must make equal offers to all customers, but there's no law that says they have to tell you about it. Usually all they require is that you asterisk their trade name with a registration notation and possibly use a specific type form.

Another type of co-op campaign is when you get together with a few compatible establishments for an ad campaign featuring a grouping of your products with theirs. For instance, one of the beer companies got together with the Seafood Council and featured a campaign of "Lobster and Lowenbrau." If you are a store, get together with neighboring stores to bring traffic to your location. Or put together a "look" campaign—your shoes, their shirts, someone else's suits, and so on. It gives you extra exposure and extra dollars, but be sure that the people you run with are in your league. Don't tie in with lesser products or stores; make sure you are in an environment of peers or betters.

PURCHASING TECHNIQUES 5

The trauma of buying intangibles

"Two hundred and fifty dollars for preparation of that little ad? And what's a mechanical and a velox, anyway?"

When you don't know what you're buying, you can feel put upon even when the bill is eminently fair. That sort of misunderstanding between supplier and client can cripple advertising and sales-promotional efforts.

It's hard for a businessman who deals in concrete objects to understand the basis for bills for intangibles such as talent and creativity. Manufacturing a handbag, now that's easy to price: so much for raw materials, so much for labor, so much for overhead, commissions—and there's your price. And look at what you've got—a solid, beautiful product that you can use, touch, and enjoy. On the other hand some cut-up pieces of paper with words pasted on a board—something called a mechanical—what's it worth?

Let's start with an explanation of what goes into the creation and production of advertising to give you some idea of what you're paying for—and then, later along, some sense of how those prices are calculated. So that you understand all the items you will find listed on your advertising bills, here is an informal glossary of the terms used in ad preparation.

GLOSSARY OF OFT-USED AD TERMS

AA's: Author's alterations. This means changes that originated from you, due either to your original errors or to later corrections and additions.

Benday: A screen process that is applied to black type or black areas to make them grey. Various gradations of greys can be achieved this way, from very light to almost black. It is a method of getting a two-tone effect from one color ink.

Binding: Stitching together pages into a catalog or booklet. Stapled, wire-bound, or plastic-bound are the most common techniques.

Bleed: When the printed area goes right up to the edge, as though it runs off the page. This costs more in printing or in media advertising, because it involves printing on more of the paper.

Blueprint: The proofs supplied in offset printing. It can show only one color, blue, but is usually adequate to judge if everything is properly placed.

Camera-ready: Completed artwork, ready for the printer to set before his camera to convert into printing negatives and plates.

Coated stock: Paper with a shiny finish. It comes coated on one or both sides.

Comp: A comprehensive of a design for presentation. It usually means a fairly tight rendering of what the finished piece of advertising will look like. Some of the comps I've seen look even better than the finished project. Comps are submitted to the client for projected ads, direct mail, literature, displays. If it's a true comp, it costs, because much time is spent in its preparation. So if you can stretch your imagination a little and settle for a "rough" (which is a primitive version of a comp), you'll save a bundle.

Die-cutting: Mechanically cutting cardboard or paper into shapes. When you want anything other than square, straight edges, it must be die-cut.

Font: A whole typeface—from A to Z. Each style of type is called a font.

Galley proofs: Sheets of rough paper that show all the set type you ordered, but not yet set up into proper page form. When doing a catalog or booklet that will undergo many revisions, it's wise to ask the typographer for galley proofs first. It's cheaper to make corrections at this early stage than it is after the type has been set up into page form.

Halftone: Printed reproduction of a photograph. It requires tone patterns and screening and special negatives. In printing, price is affected by the number of halftones included in a job.

Laid finish: A fine finish to paper. You see a nice pattern effect of vertical and horizontal lines.

Layout: The design for any piece of advertising.

Line copy: Typography is line copy; black-and-white drawings are line copy. Any composition of solid black without gradations of tone is line copy.

Lithography: Another word for offset printing.

Logo: Short for logotype. The distinctive design symbol or style of type associated with the company name.

Matte finish: Dull-finish paper.

Mechanical: Finished board with camera-ready art in place.

Mezzotint: A line print made from a photograph. It makes the picture look like an etching—very arty and effective.

Multilith: An inexpensive process of printing up to 8½-in. × 11-in. pieces in small quantities. Not recommended when a quality look is sought, since halftones always come out weaker and missing detail and sharpness.

Paste-up: Another word for mechanical.

Pica: Unit of measurement used in typesetting and printing. Six picas equal one inch.

Press proof: Proofs actually made while the job is on press. Usually used to check colors and quality of halftones. A last-minute check before the printing begins.

Production: This is the work involved in transforming a design into reality. It covers specifying sizes and styles of type, getting the type set and back to you and pasted up, arranging for photostats, photographs, and veloxes—in short, pulling together all the elements required to produce an ad or piece of advertising material.

Repros: The usual term for the typographer's glossy sheets of camera-ready type.

Retouching: Airbrushing photographs to blow out the eyesores and sharpen the strong points. Almost every photo needs a bit of retouching to provide highlights the camera may have overlooked or to straighten ragged edges that the camera did not overlook.

Reverses: The white-on-black areas in printing, as when white type appears against a black background.

Rough: A rough version of a layout. Not as fancy and exact as a comp. The words may be designated as just lines and the photos as sort of shaped smears. A rough is usually quite adequate for visualizing the finished product.

Saddle-stitching: Binding with wire staples, as used in most magazines.

Screens: The coarseness or refinement in the density of a halftone is determined by its screen number; 150 screen is finer than 85 screen. The number describes the dots per linear inch. (If you look at any printed photograph through a magnifying glass, you will see the dots.) Those used for newspapers, 55 to 85 screens, are coarser. For printing fine-quality halftones in magazines and literature, 100 to 150 screens are used.

Serifs and sans serifs: A serif typeface has a little stroke projecting from the top and bottom of each letter. A sans serif has none.

Silhouette halftone: When the tonal background is completely deleted and only the subject is shown against a solid of black, white, or color. This silhouetting can be done right on the photograph or by the printer.

Silk screen: A form of stencil printing used on cardboard or wood. Used primarily for signs and displays.

Square halftone: When the photograph is printed as is, in a square or rectangular shape.

Stuffer: Small circular for stuffing in invoice envelopes. Usually supplied by manufacturers gratis to retailers for distribution to the store customers.

Tear sheet: The magazine page containing your ad. Supplied free by the publication.

Vandyke: Same as a blueprint, only in brown ink instead of blue.

Velox: Print of a photograph which has been screened before it reaches the printer. It saves you the higher expense involved when the printer does the screening. However, if you don't have a skilled velox maker in your area, let the printer do it. A poor quality velox can kill your details and result in a murky halftone.

CREATIVITY—THE INTANGIBLE

They don't sell paintings by the pound. The value of a creative effort is not measured by size or weight.

When you buy a layout, copy, or design, you are paying for three things:

1. Time the artist or writer spent creating the concept.
2. Actual hours expended in physical execution of the idea.
3. Years spent developing the talent to produce this creative effort.

The first item—creative time—is not computed with a stopwatch, of course. That would be insanity, since some ideas come in seconds, and some take days to jell. You cannot put a meter on the brain. The second item is evaluated on a time basis. However, it is the third point that makes up the bulk of the price.

Many years ago my father demurred at a bill for $100 presented to him by the medical specialist who paid a ten-minute visit to our home and diagnosed my brother's illness as mononucleosis. My father said, "But, Doctor, $100 for only ten minutes?"

The doctor answered, "Ten minutes here, yes, but what about the 30 years of training and experience that qualified me to make that ten-minute diagnosis?"

It's the years of working with accounts and learning what approach sells, what customers want to know that will make them buy, what merchandising elements must be considered, how your sales story should be presented to get the greatest possible mileage—those are the intangibles that make the difference.

A new client once complained to me about the costs of preparing a series of ads and compared them to lower bills he had received from the ad agency he had recently left. So we compared the former ads to the new ones.

The products were English riding wear. The old ads used line drawings (cheaper to reproduce than photographs) that looked as though they had been done in a high-school art-class exercise. The new ads used high-style photographs of the boots and breeches in action. The old ad for rubber riding boots showed a pair of boots and was headed, "Protection in the Rain," which automatically restricted sales of these boots to the rainy day category.

Our ad for the same boots showed them on a young rider, sitting on a stable fence against a grey, but not rainy, sky. The ad was headed, "All weather that looks like all leather." Here was an immediate expansion of sales horizons by indicating that these smart-looking boots not only are for sloshing about in the rain, but are handsome footwear to be worn with pride in rain, snow, sun, or anytime.

The client looked at both ads side by side, and then we asked the critical question: "Which ad sold more boots?" He just smiled and never brought up the comparison-price business again.

I am not saying that you must expect or accept any price. That kind of blank-check ordering is for millionaires or fools, or both. You are entitled to, and certainly should ask for, an estimate on any creative effort.

We have basic prices for layout, copy, production, and mechanicals for an 8½-in. × 11-in. piece, an 11-in. × 17-in. piece, and so on. By now, we pretty much know how long it should take from start to finish and have it priced accordingly. Sometimes it takes longer, and we lose a little. Sometimes it goes faster, and we win a little. It all evens out in the long run. Most advertising agencies have set figures for their services that vary according to the calibre of the talent employed, and thus inevitably, the quality of the work produced.

HOW TO TELL GOOD FROM BAD WHEN BUYING ADVERTISING SERVICES

Printing

A well-printed piece is like a well-turned-out woman: You know she looks great, but you can't figure out just why. It's all a matter of skilfully, subtly executed details. However, if you examine the piece closely, you will notice that (1) the photographs are sharply defined and sparkling with contrast; (2) the colors are solid and strong, the red is really red, the black is pure black; (3) the register is right, which means that solid areas butt up to each other perfectly—there's no overlap that causes fuzzy, sloppy-looking edges.

A poorly printed piece has been run through the press fast. That's how it can have a lower price; press-time charges can be lower. Photos and colors are usually somewhat muddy. They use inexpensive inks that dry fast without giving good solid coverages. They've skimped on the calibre of the printing negatives, so you get dull, grey halftones. And there's often an irregularity in the quality of all the printed material delivered. Since they can't always afford to wait for the full colors to come through on the ink rollers before they start the run, the first batches that come off the press may not have perfect ink coverage and may look pale.

There can be a large disparity in prices between a good printer and a cheap house. I am not recommending one over the other, because not every piece requires high-quality printing, and not everyone cares. But there is a standard of quality below which no company should go. There's a large difference between a functional, commercial piece of literature and a shoddy one. You are poorly represented by a shoddy one. Ask for estimates before you buy, and ask for samples of the printer's work, so that before you decide on the cheaper source, you will be aware of how much the savings will cost you.

Photography

A good photographer will fuss with lighting and with lenses. He'll take time to position the subject intelligently. He will recognize which imperfections will be exposed by the camera's merciless eye. He has an eye for composition and will produce a nicely balanced shot.

A poor photographer, due to ignorance, laziness, or inability to take time, will not bother to do anything more than set your product in front of the camera, turn on the existing bank of lights, and shoot. The results: (1) The unpretty guts of the product show; (2) the irregular stitching that he could have turned to hide is glaringly obvious; (3) the deliveryman's greasy thumbprints have not been wiped off.

The difference in price between a good commercial photographer and a poor one is negligible—maybe no more than $10 for a product shot. Any saving is lost when you pay the bill for retouching to make the photo usable.

Sometimes it's not even price. Photography is a talent; one person has it, and the other just doesn't. So before you select a commercial photographer, take a minute to look over his samples. See if the photos are sharp, artistic, and flattering. When you give him his first assignment, go to his studio to supervise and guide. Point out what facets of the subject are to be stressed and which played down. He can't possibly know, for example, that the unfinished raw-looking edge of a pot is really a chip-resistant rim that is your big selling feature. Also, perhaps you want the box to be included.

The studio is the preferred place to shoot, since the best lighting equipment is there. However, if you have heavy machinery that is unfeasible to transport, or if you have a large number of awkward objects to photograph, it might be more convenient to have the photographer come to your place to shoot. The photos will rarely turn out as well, since the lighting is only functional and the backgrounds are usually ghastly—but if you must, you must.

Once you have established relations with a photographer and he gets to know what you want, you can just send stuff over with a very rough sketch, and more than likely, you will get satisfactory results.

There are all kinds of specialists in photography: fashion, location, food, architecture, aerial, and so on. If you're fortunate, you will find one fellow who is competent in all the areas you need. I say "competent" because there's almost no ceiling to photography charges. There are photographers who ask, and get, a thousand dollars for a single shot. I watched one of the world's most famous photographers work over the shooting of a piece of IBM equipment for hours, and he told me that he had been at it since the previous day. Just an ordinary little grey desk-top machine, and each photo that he had discarded looked like a minor masterpiece to me. Still, he wasn't satisfied. But then, IBM could afford to pay for the photographer's indulging himself in the luxury of achieving perfection.

For small business use, genius is not a requirement. Just reasonable talent and competence.

Photo Retouching

It's usually necessary to retouch a photo somewhat—just a bit of airbrushing here and there to deaden or delineate detail. The better the photograph, the less retouching needed, of course. But when it is necessary, make sure you find a retoucher who has a *light* touch. That's the quality that makes the difference. A skilled artist airbrushes smoothly graduated tones and subtle highlights, so that the retouching is almost impossible to detect; you just end up with a clear, sharp, beautiful photograph. An unskilled retoucher will go heavy on the white paint, will leave strong blocks of dark color, and will make highlights look like white streaks. You end up with a clunky picture that more resembles a rendering than a photograph.

Remember that there are specialists in retouching as well as in photography. Some are great with machinery but can turn humans into death masks. Just be sure you have the right artist for the job.

TO BARGAIN OR NOT TO BARGAIN

Many commercial entrepreneurial types think it's shrewd to play the heavy businessman when dealing with artists or agencies. They bargain; they haggle. If the artist quotes $350, they drive the price down to $300 and feel a sense of businesslike achievement.

But it doesn't work. Bargaining is a bust with a creative source. You are dealing with a creative person whose work may be much affected by your approach. Basically, every artist aims to please himself. He'll work and rework to get a result that comes up to his personal standards. Antagonize him at the outset, and you will get first-draft "off the top of the head" thinking. He won't bother with the all-important refinement processes—he won't begrudge you the time.

That doesn't mean that you shouldn't ask for an estimate or admit that it's more than you are prepared to spend. For example, you might have a limited budget for a specific project. There's no harm in announcing,

Drab and Dull: Here we are dealing with a photographer who has no eye, no patience, and no talent. The pieces were just plopped on a table under the existing lighting and shot. The products are spread out unnecessarily so that everything appears small and out of focus. The most important and salable features of the china—the pattern and contours—are lost due to the poor arrangement and camera angles. Everything looks flat because the poor lighting highlights only the items introduced as accents—the apple and spoon. Another cardinal error: the teapot is pointed out of the photo rather than bringing the eye into it.

Smart and Sparkling: Can you believe this photographer was dealing with exactly the same elements? Note how the china seems larger, lovelier, and more important. It's all in the arrangement and lighting and indicates a skilled eye and hand. By grouping everything closely together, he has created a larger and more cohesive picture. The graceful contours of the handles and lids are clearly visible, as is the all-important pattern of the china on each piece. The touch of silverware and linen napkin do their job of creating an ambiance. Notice how everything shines.
(Photography by Jerry Finzi Studio, New York, NY)

STEP-BY-STEP ADVERTISING

"Look, I have just $500 for art. Can you do it for that price?" That's perfectly reasonable, and the artist has the option to turn you down if he finds the price impossible. Chances are, if you have developed a rapport and need a special price, he'll happily accommodate, providing you don't pull that poor-mouth too often. Once you have a working relationship with an artist, agency, photographer, or printer, and you know the prices are fair, don't haggle. It only creates an ill will that will blow you absolutely no good.

AVOIDING SHAMEFUL WASTE

We have a morgue of dead roughs: It's my heartbreak file of clever copy and gorgeous graphics that died unborn because of that very expensive type of client exercise—mind-changing.

It's a very costly activity and one you should try to avoid. There's nothing more disheartening and wasteful then spending hours in the creation of a promotion, an ad, a mailer—whatever—only to have the client call to advise that due to circumstances entirely within his control, he no longer needs the piece, or he wants it in an entirely different form. He gets charged for the unused work, and it's a total loss to all. Here are some examples of wastes that could have been avoided:

"What we need is a big brochure that shows the whole line, so the salesmen can carry it around instead of our big catalog."

Fine. The agency prepares the layout and copy, and sends out the rough for the client to look over.

Then comes the call.

"Er-er . . . we showed the rough to our salesmen and they say it's nice, but they have to carry the big catalog anyway. So I guess we really don't need the brochure."

Why the devil didn't he check with the salesmen before? It's not nice to call the client an idiot, so you mutter something clever about that being the way the cookie crumbles, and you hang up wondering why you didn't go into some other profession.

If you think an ad piece is needed, check first with those you think need it *before* you give out the assignment.

"Big news. We've just set up a free-call direct line to our factory to speed up customer-service inquiries. Make up a big mailing right away."

The piece gets finished and ready for camera, and then comes the phone call.

"Er-er." (Clients usually stammer when they're wrong, I'll say that for them.) "We just realized we don't want to push the free phone bit or we'll have every chiseller phoning in orders instead of mailing them. Just change the emphasis on the piece. Tell 'em to send their orders right to the plant, and mention the free phone casually."

Those little words "change the emphasis" translated into ad language mean "Do the whole piece over."

If it's something new, think it through *before* you give out the assignment.

Communicate. That's the most important waste preventative of all. If you have something special in mind, take the time to convey it. Even though most advertising folk are talented, perceptive, and sensitive, mind reading is not one of the standard trade attributes.

Often you will have a mental image of what you would like to see in a printed piece, a design, a photo, and will tend to judge the result by how close it comes to your preconception. In those situations, take a piece of paper and draw a rough of what you have in mind. I can hear the howls of pain and protest: "Me? Draw? I'm all thumbs. All I can draw are conclusions." No one is expecting a Rembrandt, just a rough that is enough to convey a feeling. This sort of little sketch, no matter how primitive, can be an invaluable guide that may save you and the creative source time and money.

Communicate your ideas graphically. No matter how primitive, it can do the job.

THE "NEW CORPORATE IMAGE" CRAZE

There comes a moment in the development of every small business when someone says, "What we need is a constant corporate image, a continuity in all our promotional output."

That someone is usually the new sales manager or marketing manager. He's been brought in to beef up sales, to pull together all the amorphous efforts and activities that had been previously handled by a dozen different unqualified people to whom the jobs had fallen by default.

The new man is usually hit all at once with the results of ten years of corporate chaos. He finds he has the bewildering, overwhelming task of converting near-anarchy into a disciplined organization. At about this point one of the corporate-image vendors approaches him with the proposal for a complete evaluation of the corporate image and the evolution of a total graphics approach that will make it all hang together.

The poor fellow falls upon the suggestion as if he has found his Rosetta

STEP-BY-STEP ADVERTISING

stone. It sounds so logical, so comforting—so impressively big business. So he stumps for it to management and proclaims that the process will be the panacea for all their ills and that, in one step, it will erase the corrosion of years of corporate confusion.

If he wins, the company pays for anywhere from five thousand to ten thousand dollars, and the corporate-image vendors do their stuff.

They usually claim that they must go out into the field and do research studies to get a feel for the market before the proper concept can be achieved. Time passes, sketches are submitted, and ultimately they produce a new "individualized, powerful logo"—maybe a stylized rendition of the first letter of the company name or some graphic gimmick to convey the firm's field of endeavor. (The original logo which the company has been using for years may or may not be old-fashioned. That's not always bad. Often it's distinctive, and more importantly, everyone recognizes it—that's what you want.)

The new logo is hailed as the new cohesive factor in the company and necessitates redesigned letterheads, labels, and packaging. Then comes the recommendation that all company literature and packaging feature a strong familial relationship. Result: good taste and guaranteed monotony.

I'm all for good packaging, but where is it written that they must all look alike or even similar? Nobody buys a product because it looks like another. Every sale is made based on the appeal of that individual item. The only one who truly appreciates a family similarity in packaging is the boss, because it gives him a good feeling to see such a nice, neatly coordinated stock room.

If you will note the packaging of leading consumer products, everyone is handled as an individual product. Resemblance is scrupulously avoided. The name of the game is to stand out, not blend into a shelf of look-alikes.

As for the brand-new logo, do you really think that Westinghouse sales skyrocketed because they paid Paul Rand a fortune to produce the distinctive "W"?

The expenditure of thousands of dollars on a "new corporate image and logo" is a type of indulgence favored by new executives of giant corporations who have money to toss around and a need to justify their new positions. I have never seen any documentation or proof to indicate that a new logo produces profit for anyone but the graphic designers, printers, and packaging companies. For the small business, such a project is a useless, nonproductive extravagance.

COPYWRITING 6

How to write an ad that sells

Advertising is somewhat like architecture in one vital respect. The value of the work is judged, not for itself, but for its effectiveness in achieving a specific purpose.

Lincoln Center's Avery Fisher Hall in New York City is a classic example of award-winning beauty that didn't work at first. A stunning edifice, comfortable facilities, fine visibility. Only one thing wrong—you couldn't hear the music well.

How many times have you admired an ad for its cleverness, its outstanding graphics, and then ten minutes later, realized you didn't know what the ad was selling? This sort of fiasco is usually the product of a series of Madison Avenue mutual-massaging-of-the-ego sessions. Its prime motive, for the creators, is to win accolades from their peers. The client is expected to bask in their reflected glory and pride of artistic achievement when his company's ad wins an award.

We of the small budgets consider this the lowest form of sophistry. In our pragmatic world the success of any ad is measured by one yardstick only: sales. Advertising art is never for art's sake; it is solely for the sake of motivating people to buy.

There is a classic advertising agency ad that has been repeated time and time again over the past 25 years. It shows two identical photos of a man sitting in an armchair reading a newspaper. The first picture is captioned: "Gosh, this is a great ad!" The second picture is captioned: "Gosh, this is a great product!" The explanation beneath both, of course, indicates that this ad agency supports the second position. So do I. So must you.

Basic copywriting rule 1: You can be creative and clever in smaller-budget advertising. But none of these aims must be allowed to overshadow the prime purpose of the ad—*to sell.*

SMALL AND HONEST

There's no doubt that people are impressed and somewhat cowed by four-color double-page spreads. Bigness conveys wealth, wealth means success, and success means they're good—or how else did they get so big?

That's the big hurdle in smaller-budget advertising—to convey solidity and reliability in a big way but in small space.

As every con man knows, if you want to hook a mark, do it big. Most people have an implicit trust in vastness. That's why the con-type ads are usually big and flashy. Everyone has undoubtedly seen the ads that sell palm-tree-studded sites in some Florida swamp, or the ads that offer inflatable overalls to deflate overweight. Notice they all go in for full-page ads in the high-priced media. They have to.

When you have something solid and reliable to sell, you can do it very successfully in more modest space. However, since you do not have the credibility factor of bigness to impress the reader with, you must do it with absolute honesty. No overstated claims, no lavish promises, no implausible statements. Once a shred of disbelief enters the reader's mind, the entire ad crumbles. The big guys can afford a little exaggeration here and there, but you can't. Like Caesar's wife, you have to be above suspicion.

Basic copywriting rule 2: In small businesses, honesty is not the best policy—it is the only policy. Dramatize, elaborate, but never overrate or overstate.

HOW TO WRITE COPY THAT SELLS

It isn't difficult to write copy that sells, and it really doesn't require great genius. The most important part of writing good copy is evolving the right approach, the basic appeal that touches closest to the heart of the buyer. It is a distillation process, a careful analysis of the product or service you are selling and of the needs of the people who will be buying it.

Step 1: Analyze your product or service. Evaluate its features, and list every conceivable service it performs for the user. For example, you have a laundry: You turn out finely finished work; you pick up and deliver;

you replace broken and lost buttons. You have a local gift shop: You carry a highly selective group of items from leading manufacturers as well as an eclectic array of contemporary handicrafts. You manufacture lamps: You feature a special patented-design light that has spring-controlled extending arms. You manage a local bank: You offer many loan services plus personalized advice on family finance and money management. You distribute plumbing supplies: You carry a huge stock of the best lines available; you guarantee shipment the same day an order is received.

Step 2: Translate these product features into terms of user benefits. Now that you know what your product does, figure out what tangible benefits these features mean to potential buyers. Nobody much cares that your product or service is great unless they know what great things it can do for them. You must sell the benefit, not the product.

Following up on the previous examples, let's start with the laundry. What can your finely finished work, pickup and delivery, and button-sewing service mean to the housewife? Answer: (1) tremendous convenience, (2) more leisure time, (3) a happier husband (fewer complaints), and (4) a smoother home life.

The gift shop: What can your eclectic array of gifts mean to the shopper? Answer: (1) elimination of the wear and tear of travelling downtown, (2) the convenience of one-stop shopping for all gifts.

The lamp manufacturer: What benefits can a lamp that stretches bring to a user? Answer: (1) ideal for children who like to squirm about when reading, (2) gives them better light, better studying conditions.

The local bank: What does the personal touch of dealing with a local bank mean? Answer: (1) It's easier to get a loan because the bank knows you and your standing in the community; (2) you avoid the unpleasant hat-in-hand position when you walk in cold to a strange bank.

The plumbing distributor: What can your high-quality merchandise and fast delivery mean to the local plumber? Answer: (1) confidence that he won't get complaints about equipment after he has installed it, (2) better, faster service to his customers as a result of immediate delivery.

Basic copywriting rule 3: Evaluate your products, and translate the benefits into values the customer can readily identify with. Don't just think of what the product does, but what it does for the user.

Step 3: Now that you have assembled your arsenal of facts and the slant to be used, it is time to arrange it in ad form.

For the headline, take your prime user benefit, and convert it into as succinct a statement as you can. Tell it, and tell it fast. For instance, here are some possibilities: The laundry: "We free you for the better things in life." The gift shop: "The Right Gift ... in the Right Place ... Right here on Main Street." The lamp manufacturer: "The Activist—the lamp that follows the student movement." The bank: "Of course we'll help out with money. That's what neighbors are for!" The plumbing distributor: "Order Today—Install Tomorrow."

These are just some suggestions to give you an idea of procedure. If you think about them and doodle about a bit, you will come up with dozens of possible headlines for these ad situations. They don't all have to be declarative statements; questions are great stoppers. But try it; it's good exercise, and it gets your mind moving into the right channels for copywriting.

As real-life postscripts to the hypothetical situations I've used above, here are some actual headline approaches that proved highly successful. When our client came out with one of the first word processors, we planned ads to reach office managers. We tried to think of what problems these fantastic machines would solve for the office manager, and in what ways he would be made to look like a hero—everyone wants to look like a hero, especially to his boss. And how could we phrase the benefits in an easily identifiable frame of reference, dealing with the day-to-day problems the office manager must face?

The headline that did it was "How to get 65 hrs. of typing from every 35-hr.-a-week typist."

Since office managers have trouble these days getting 20 hours of work from a 35-hour-a-week typist, the headline was a real grabber. Also, the use of the word "every" indicated that no special training was required to operate the machine; every typist could handle it.

The Environmental Farms of Tucson had developed a new kind of tomato that was being grown in the most fantastically controlled conditions science and nature could produce. Because of their carefully nurtured situation, they could be picked ripe (instead of green) and flown to market within a day.

Now, how to convey, in a headline, that here was a new, luscious, extraordinarily tasty tomato?

"Introducing ... the brand-new vegetable/fruit tomato," with a picture of a wholesome young girl biting into it as you would an apple. What was instantly conveyed was: Here's a unique tomato that's as sweet and delicious as a piece of fruit. This headline became the company slogan and went into all their ads and on packaging as well.

COPYWRITING

Okay, you've stopped the reader with your headline. What do you do next? You sell him with the body of the ad. You enumerate all the advantages your headline has promised, in short, terse sentences, with no wasted words. Keep it spare, keep it lean, and keep it direct.

After you have written a first draft, go over it again and again to weed out all the unnecessary words. It's easy to write a long ad; what's hard is to produce a short one. Don't be afraid to use phrases and incomplete sentences. Your fifth-grade teacher isn't around to fault you on grammar and to insist on perfectly formed syntax. Sometimes the use of a phrase gives a nice clipped pace that makes for easier reading. For example, "It's a handsome coat. And lightweight, too." Somehow that looks better and reads faster than: "It's a handsome coat, and it is lightweight, too."

They're primed, they're convinced; they want whatever it is you're selling. What do they do now to get it? Now comes the hook.

Never, *never* write an ad, a sales letter, a presentation, any piece of advertising, without in some way instructing the reader on the step he or she must take to see or buy or get further facts about the product. Any advertising that omits this basic information is a waste of the reader's time and a waste of the advertiser's money.

Decide what action you want them to take, and ask them to do it. If you want inquiries so that you can pass the sales leads on to your salesmen, ask them to write in for literature. If you want them to go out and buy the product, tell them where. If you want them to send in an order, ask them to do it at once.

Whatever you want the readers to do, *tell them plainly at the bottom of the ad.* If you can offer some special incentive to motivate them to act immediately, before they put the ad aside and possibly forget it, so much the better. And make it a limited offer: "Good only until. . . ." This sort of pressure can impel the reader to act now, and that's what you want.

"Bring in this ad and get $1.00 off."

"Order now and get a free gift."

"Buy now while the special price sale is on."

Basic copywriting rule 4: Don't be bashful; ask for the order.

SUPPLEMENTARY COPYWRITING TIPS

Use Humor

The light touch can be very effective—unless you're selling burial plots. It suspends disbelief and makes you more likable and somewhat more credible. Most people, as you know, mistrust advertising statements. A bit of humor that shows you are real people, not some pompous corporate body, lowers the anti-advertising guard a bit, and allows acceptance to sneak in.

There are lots of ways to use humor. If you have an odd name, you can turn it into an asset by owning up to it and treating it lightly. "With a name like Smuckers, it's got to be good," is a prime example.

Or you can show comic-tragic situations people can get themselves into when they do not use your product, such as that great series of ads by Talon that portrayed the embarrassing positions one can be caught in when a critical zipper breaks.

Puns can be attention-getting. We once used what could be a dreadful pun, because it was going to a pun-appreciative audience. We were promoting an academic-year calendar to college students. The aim of the piece was to point out the hazards of being unaware of days and dates. The heading was, "Summa Cum Later," which may make you wince but made them buy a lot of calendars.

If you have an uninteresting product, humor can take the curse off it. If the medium you are using, or the market you are hitting, is burdened with dull, super-serious material (ever look through some of the engineering magazines?), an injection of lightness can make your ad stand out.

Don't Fuss over Quality

Just as every mother tells you that her child is the greatest, so every seller announces that his product is the best. Both of these statements, when made publicly, are considered equally objective and equally believable.

How many times have I asked a client, "In what ways is your product better?" and gotten the answer: "In every way. It's the finest-quality product in the industry."

In many cases it may be perfectly true, but general statements of excellence are totally unconvincing. That doesn't mean that you should ignore the quality factor. Not at all—it's very important. However the only way to convey superiority and get some credibility is with specific claims. Select particular features, individual aspects that you can point up, and then translate them into the direct benefits the buyer will derive from these higher-quality factors.

For example, if you are selling English riding breeches that are made by England's finest tailors, you could just state that fact: "Tailored by England's finest riding-wear craftsmen." Nice. Dignified. But so what? This type of statement usually pleases the manufacturer because it has the classy ring he likes. Rarely does it have any effect on prospective purchasers. Not unless you distill the fact into what it can mean to the user: "Incredibly cut by England's finest tailors to give you a marvellous figure and freedom." Now you have told purchasers why these breeches are superior and how the superiority affects them.

Sometimes lack of quality is an asset—*if* you make a deliberate point of it and it is a part of your selling story. For example, a client produced cassette transports which computer manufacturers integrate into their units. These transports were of very simple, thus less expensive, construction and performed limited functions. They were designed for users who needed only those limited functions but who up to now had been forced to buy costly, complicated units that offered services they could not use. The lack of quality, reflected in the lower price, was its greatest selling asset.

"Why pay for overcapability?" was the theme of the campaign.

Avoiding the big stress on top quality is sometimes difficult in the arena of small business. You usually deal with the founders of the company, the people who actively were involved in its creation and development. Their feelings towards the firm are strongly emotional. They have worked on every facet of its growth and believe implicitly that their product is the very finest of its kind.

Being more objective and having the advantage of dealing with many companies, I know that there is rarely any one finest of its kind. Usually there are a few of comparable excellence, each having different points of superiority. So if you are the company principal, please heed these words; they can save you a lot of money in wasted advertising space: Nobody really cares how well you make your product. All they want to know is how well your product will work for them.

Appeal to Emotional Needs

When you are evaluating product benefits, don't overlook the aspects that satisfy emotional needs. These are very powerful sales motivators.

Self-image, snob appeal, peer approval, and the like can be a big driving force in the marketplace. People buy Cadillacs and Mercedes not only because they like driving them; they like owning them. If your product or service is an instrument of prestige, play it up.

STEP-BY-STEP ADVERTISING

If you were promoting a school that trained people for specific fields and professions, you would, of course, mention the greater income rewards that could lie ahead. More importantly, stress the prestige factors connected to their new positions: the alteration in community image when they move from blue collar to white, the sort of people they might hobnob with.

One of the big motivational research organizations once came out with the tidbit that a convertible automobile represented a mistress to the male buyer. Now there's an emotional need. You may not find one quite as primordial for your product, but it never hurts to try.

If you have an art gallery, you might hint at the cultural quality original art imparts to one's home. If you sell books, you might indicate the intellectual cachet that well-stocked bookshelves can give one, and the greater social acceptance one will have on being able to converse about the information acquired from the books.

"Be the first on your block" and other appeals to status can have a mighty big pull.

Remember Greed

The profit motive—that's the greatest buying consideration when you are selling to dealers. If someone is buying your product to resell it at a profit, then the bigger the profit, the bigger his buying incentive.

If your profit margin is larger than usual, if you offer an extra discount, if you have proof that your merchandise can be moved off the shelves faster, if you are planning to back up your product with an extensive TV campaign that will surely build a huge demand, *tell them.*

But please, if you do not offer any of these higher-profit advantages, don't claim you do because you think it sounds like the right thing to say. If you have no facts to back up your claim, you'll only destroy your credibility and the positive effect of your ad.

Avoid Invisible Phrases

There are a host of advertising clichés that I call the invisible phrases because they are so overused that nobody really sees them. The eye just glides over the words without bothering to notify the brain.

Pick up any trade magazine, and count how many times you see these hackneyed expressions:

Fast turnover   Fast service
Impulse-buy item   Pioneers in the industry
Outstanding quality   Leaders in the field

Ad nauseam. Avoid them. They are a total waste of space. If you cannot communicate these ideas in a more specific, effective way, don't.

Don't Let Dignity Dull Dynamics

One of the frequent problems I've run into with the small entrepreneur is his supersensitivity to his dignity, whatever that means. I guess it's like the old story of the millionaire who dresses like a bum. He can afford to. When a rich man wears sneakers with his tuxedo, they call him eccentric. But let some poor oaf dress that way, and he's immediately labelled a slob.

That's the image that troubles the little fellow in business. He's afraid to do anything daring or innovative for fear of being accused of cheapness. It reminds me of a party I attended where the bar featured an assortment of anonymous brand liquor. After a few belts, one of the guests advised the host, in ringing tones: "Joel, you're not rich enough to serve such cheap Scotch."

There is, after all, some validity to the smaller business owner's concern with image. As we discussed earlier, he cannot risk dishonesty, and he cannot risk exaggeration. But dignity? There's nothing more stuffy, stultifying, and deadly dull than dignity.

If you allow the misguided belief that dramatic dynamics cannot coexist with dignity in advertising, then you'll be turning out the quickest-to-hit-the-wastebasket material ever produced.

The main object of any piece of promotion is to sell—and subliminally, to convey a corporate image of solidity and reliability. In order to get anyone to read your message, you must first capture his attention, and you can't do that with dignity. I don't mean that you should use garish design or nudes. That's lack of taste, not lack of dignity.

Remember, creativity and innovativeness convey the image of an aggressive, progressive, live organization, and that's the sort of stuff that moves merchandise.

Direct mail 7

The "now" medium

Whether it comes from a laundry or a foundry, from a cemetery or a caterer, there's one thing all direct mail pieces have in common: They aim to induce the recipient to *act now*.

There should be an immediacy about direct mail, an urgency that impels the reader to run out and buy right now. That is its purpose. Print advertising (newspapers and magazines), television, and radio are used to inform the public that you have a great thing that they cannot seriously contemplate living without and to tell them how to get to the point of purchase.

Direct mail tells the same tale, but it gives people the mechanism for immediate ordering. If your piece is effective, people will be primed to purchase at once, and the order cards will flow.

That's what your direct mail is supposed to achieve. If the customer reads it.

Too many companies lull themselves into believing that the whole world out there is just dying for their product or service. One of our clients assures us, constantly and solemnly, that all the people on his mailing list will read any printed material that bears his company name, due to the tremendous respect the entire industry has for his firm. Companies have gone bankrupt on such delusions.

The fact is, nobody reads any third-class mail unless you cleverly provoke his interest, hit him in the bankbook, or both. If you want your di-

DIRECT MAIL

rect mail to work well for you, it must be attention-getting. Mailing has become incredibly expensive these days, what with postage increases, mailing-house costs, and the like. No small company can afford to waste what is now big money on unread, ineffective mailings.

When you use direct mail, it must be well planned and professionally executed. Don't be tempted to ask your neighbor's son, whom everyone claims is another Picasso and who has won the local Halloween window-painting contest three years running.

Even if you are a local service or store or restaurant, mailings shouldn't look homemade. Remember that when a mailing arrives at its destination, whether a domestic or a business mailbox, it will be competing with some pretty jazzy-looking material. True, if everyone else's piece is slick, your primitive-looking mailing will stand out. That's great, but there's a big difference between primitive and crude. Too, you want to be sure that simple and primitive is the image you want to impart. That might be fine for a shop selling quaint crafts or rugged sportswear but not very beneficial for an equipment company that wants to convey precision workmanship.

There's a skill, and thus expense, involved in commercial-art preparation; this is one expense you cannot afford to bypass. Beware of circulars written and designed by local printers. They all have a way of looking like handbills announcing the day's special on ground chuck.

Ever get one of those simple little four-color mailings from Time-Life, printed on paper that costs a little less than the Hope diamond, and that opens up to modest mural size? Next time you get one, handle it with respect; it probably costs more than your whole mortgage.

How can you even begin to compete? It's easy. Since you are number 2,000, you try much harder. There are many ways to command attention that are inexpensive, ingenious, resourceful. As a matter of fact, sometimes those elaborate budget-busting jobs, with foldouts and pop-ups, are hoisted by their own petards. The recipient often gets so hung up on the sheer gorgeousness and gimmickry of the piece that he forgets just what it is they are trying to sell him.

Simple can be good. Here are some ways to achieve effectiveness by using cleverness instead of cash.

THE FAMILIAR OBJECT IN THE UNFAMILIAR PLACE

Take an object that is familiar to everyone, and use it in a totally unfamiliar place, in a startlingly unexpected way.

STEP-BY-STEP ADVERTISING

A Paper Bag

Here's one of the commonest things around: a plain paper bag. You see it at home, in the office (usually transporting coffee and a danish), but how about in with your morning mail?

You can use an ordinary paper bag as an envelope; it's a real stopper, and it works wonderfully (I know, I've used it quite successfully). You print on the outside of the bag, insert your advertising material, staple it, stamp it, and mail it. It's that simple, and extremely startling.

Of course, you don't use the bag without cleverly tying it in with your sales story. Think of the many transitional approaches you can use with "It's in the Bag."

Harkening back to the hypothetical advertisers in the previous chapter:

The laundry: "Our integrity is in the bag. You can be sure it's perfect, clean, and as you like it when it comes in a BonTon Bag."

The plumbing-supply distributor: "Sales are in the bag when your installations contain E-Z plumbing products."

These are just some ideas of the way you can use the bag to pique interest and get your sales story across entertainingly. But whatever you do, don't overdo a metaphor. Just use it for openers, drop it, and let it go at that. There's nothing more amateurish than a writer who falls in love with his own metaphor and gets so carried away that you and he both forget whatever it was he was trying to sell. The most overused category of metaphor is the sports one. You know: "We'll carry the ball," "You'll score a touchdown," "You're batting a thousand," ad nauseam, until you don't know if they're trying to sell you electrical fixtures or athlete's-foot powder.

A Bank Statement

If you were a bank and sent out a bank statement, nobody would bat an eyelash. But if you were a frozen-food distributor and sent out what looked like a bank statement, that would be startling. And it's so easy and inexpensive to do. You merely use the same color and weight paper as the usual bank statement and set it up in columns in bank style, so that it looks exactly like a bank statement. In fact, get an actual statement, and copy the style and format exactly. Except use your company name on top, of course.

Then put your selling pitch in some form that relates to a bank statement. For instance: "Want big orders to build up your $$$ deposits?

Push the New Kleer-Vu Photo Albums, guaranteed to produce a fantastically high rate of interest among your customers ..."

But absolute authenticity is the vital word here. It must look exactly like a bank statement. A looks-something-like won't do and loses the whole effect. When the recipient sees that piece on his desk or in his mailbox, he has to get the instant impression that this is an important piece of information from a bank. That means your envelope must be a plain bank-style manila window envelope, with no advertising message on front.

You can bet that envelope will be opened fast, and that means you have accomplished the first aim of direct mail—to get the receiver to *open it*.

While we're in the financial area, how about a ledger sheet? Or a simulated checkbook? Or a bank-deposit slip? They are all easy to obtain and simple to reproduce.

Just get your mind going to all the ordinary objects, which you see and handle day by day, that could be adapted for direct mail.

A Piece of Cloth

Take a piece of cloth, for example, and print your message right on it. Of course, not every printer can print on cloth. We surmounted that problem by contacting a label manufacturer. It was no problem for him to print a 6-in. × 9-in. piece of fabric, and we used an opening line something like "Maybe we can't send you from rags to riches, but ..."

It was so effective, as a matter of fact, that we used this device a number of ways. Once we used a special soft cloth and had the label manufacturer pink the edges. At the bottom of the cloth we had a little "P.S." to advise that this cloth could be used as a handy wiper for eyeglasses and should be kept. Which it was, which means our effective direct mail piece had also gained the added sales-promotional value of becoming an advertising specialty and gave prolonged life to our sales message.

A Photofinishing Bag

Developed photos always come in a small bag, right? Actually, if you look at it carefully, it is not a special bag, just an ordinary 5-in. × 8-in. envelope with an end opening. If it were blank, you would recognize it as an envelope. But print the whole front with the prescribed photofinishing pattern of boxes and notations, and—*poof!*—it's a photofinishing bag.

When you see these photo bags in the photo store or in that shoe box you shove them into when you get home, you would barely notice them. After all, that's where you expect to find them. But in among your mail at the office? Wow!

Why not send out your direct-mail piece in a simulated photofinishing envelope? There's nothing to it. Just take one of those bags out of the shoe box, send it to the envelope company, and ask them to reproduce it on the front of a 5-in. × 8-in. envelope (substituting your company name for any identifiable photofinisher). Use the other blank side for addressing, and it will be a guaranteed eye-grabber in any pile of mundane mail.

Of course, the insides of the envelope must follow up on the promise of the outside; otherwise you are obviously trying to fool the recipient with a fake device. No one likes to be fooled or feels kindly disposed towards the fooler.

(Ever find one of those simulated traffic tickets under your windshield wiper that turned out to be an advertisement? After the initial shock, when your heart has resumed its pumping so that enough blood gets to your fingers to enable them to pry the piece from under the wiper, how do you feel when you read: "Here's your ticket to carefree motoring. Drive in now to Joe's Muffler Shop for a free muffler inspection"? I know I usually feel like driving right in—at 60 miles an hour.)

THE BOLD FOLD

Take an 8½-in. × 11-in. sheet of paper—the commonest, least expensive size—and fold it twice horizontally, in the commonest style, and what have you got? A one-page letter. Predictable, unimaginative, dull.

Now take that same sheet of paper, and fold it first in half horizontally and then once vertically. What do you have? A many-paged folder, or an invitation, or an announcement, or a greeting card.

Using that same 8½-in. × 11-in. sheet, lay it horizontally on your desk, fold it accordion-style, and—*presto!*—a six- or eight-page folder.

Look at all the creative possibilities that can develop from a basic 8½-in. × 11-in. sheet. Keep it flat, handbill style, and you'd end up with just one page (and a back). Each page is viewed as a single entity and must be treated that way. The limitations are obvious: You are restricted to as much or as little as the eye can grasp in one look, and you must rely heavily on graphics to direct the eye from points of major importance to those of lesser value.

But fold the sheet, and you have panels, pages; and you can lead the reader in selective step-by-step sales-building procedure. Where before you could only effectively feature one offering on a page and attempt to convey only one concept at a look, now you can show up to eight! Not only have you made the same piece of paper work harder and do more, but you have made it look more impressive. You have endowed it with substance. It's no longer a sheet—it's a brochure.

The Invitation-style Fold

Here you can use an invitation slant: "We invite you to see the new line of ABC products—right here!"

Or as an announcement: "Announcing an entirely new concept in gift-giving." Of course, this style must be sent out in a matching-style envelope (but more on envelopes later).

The Accordion-style Fold

Fold the sheet three times, hold it vertically, and suddenly you have an eight-page folder—a miniature pocket-sized catalog. Each panel can feature a different product or service, with the front page functioning as a cover. Fold it twice if you need larger panels.

The Accordion-style Indexed-Top Fold

Take your accordion-style folder, open it, and make an angle cutoff along the long side of the sheet.

I can just hear the printing cognoscenti saying: "Aha, a die-cut. Now we blow the whole budget!"

Not so. This is a die-cut effect achieved without encountering the die-cutting cost. It never has to leave the printer and be shipped off to the time-consuming, cash-consuming die-cutter—the fellow who uses huge machinery and special dies to cut holes, angles, and shapes in paper and cardboard.

This cleverly conceived diagonal cut can be handled by any printer's standard paper-cutting equipment. He will charge for the process, but it is a pittance compared to the fancy figures you get hit with once you get involved with die-cutting. The charges they impose can double the cost of a direct-mail piece.

The effect achieved by this simple diagonal slash is to create an instant index—instantly visible at first glance. This makes an ideal presentation for many products or many points.

STEP-BY-STEP ADVERTISING

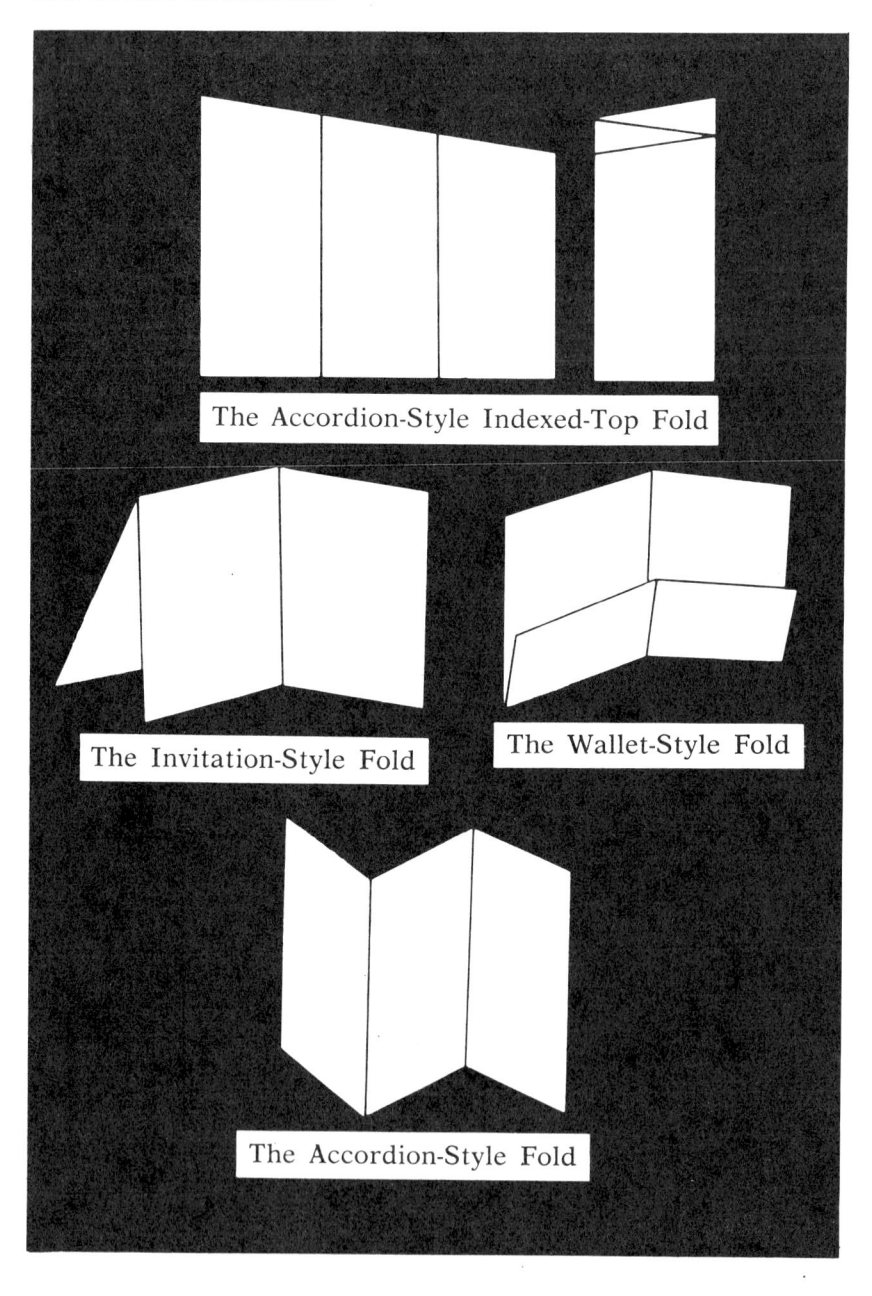

The Accordion-Style Indexed-Top Fold

The Invitation-Style Fold

The Wallet-Style Fold

The Accordion-Style Fold

The Wallet-style Fold

Department stores are particularly partial to the wallet-style fold, and it's so versatile, you wonder why no one else has adopted it.

Again it's the plain 8½-in. × 11-in. sheet. One off-center vertical fold and one horizontal fold, and you have a wallet, ready to carry a packet of individual little sheets or cards, each featuring a different product or service.

This is the ideal folder to use with the photo envelope described previously. Use a colored paper or a white paper with colored ink: "These new models are so beautiful, we felt that only pictures could do them justice." Then fill the inside pockets with miniature catalog sheets of a whole batch of products, or cards with a picture on front and details on the back.

THE ENVELOPE FOR INSTANT IMPACT

The envelope is not just a carrier of your literature; it is perhaps the most important part of your direct-mail promotion. It is your introduction—the primary attention-getting device on which your promotion can live or die. It takes you over the first vital direct-mail hurdle: getting the buyer to open it now.

The No. 10 envelope is the common garden variety used for all business correspondence. A plain white one of that size is the envelope annually elected to be the most-certain-to-be-overlooked envelope on the pile. It guarantees instant obscurity. And if you want to accelerate the movement of a direct-mail piece from desk to wastebasket, just put some lyrical message on the outside, like, "Come and get big profits now."

With that sort of provocative prose you often save the recipient the nuisance of opening the envelope; he just may toss it out at first glance.

If you must use that kind of white No. 10 for whatever reason, at least give it a fighting chance. Leave it totally blank so that you are appealing to the prospect's curiosity; he wants to know what's inside—maybe even a price decrease. (He can dream, can't he?) Given those odds, he will probably open it.

Squares, oblongs, baronials—these are just some of the more unusual envelopes available as stock items from any envelope house. Ask for a catalog of envelope styles or a list of every size and style that your envelope house carries as stock numbers.

Be sure to convey that you do not wish to be restricted to business-type envelopes. Social styles (the square baronials on rag paper) have a personal look that tempts everyone to open them.

There are many industrial-style envelopes used in factories for carrying interplant communications. There are the bank-style discussed earlier, pay envelopes, and small manila envelopes used by jewelers.

Any one of these will stand out on a pile of business correspondence. Try to use a distinctive non-run-of-the-mill style for every promotion. It helps considerably to make that important initial impact.

Sometimes you can pick up stock envelopes in bright colors. Usually color is a made-to-order job that requires a huge run, but some places have them in stock for special customers. Ask your envelope supplier. You never know.

There is a stock envelope that has a clear window almost the full size of the envelope (not just a little tiny one for the address). It comes in No. 10 size and also in a 5-in. × 8-in. size. These will display the complete cover of your mailing piece on sight. They create a picture-window effect that has the recipient reading your sales message even before he opens the envelope. What more can you ask of an envelope?

GIANT POSTCARDS—THE TRAVELLING BILLBOARDS

No envelopes to fight through. A postcard just hits the desk and spills its story straight out.

It's an instant billboard that cannot be missed. It has to be seen and can be read even as it's being thrown away.

A giant-sized card is a good way to communicate a single fact, a special announcement, a special sale, a new location, a new distributor or warehouse, and so on. Just don't get carried away and start jamming in twelve different things, or you will lose the billboard effect that is the card's only advantage.

HOW TO USE COLOR

Four-color printing is effective but not necessarily four times more effective than one-color. However, there are instances when full color does a job that really cannot be done with less; when it does not pay to produce the literature at all unless it shows the products in full color.

This is especially true with decorator and fashion merchandise: home furnishings where you feature new designs in smashing new colors, bedspreads, dresses in new fashion fabrics, or when you are presenting a new colorful line of packaging.

These things cannot be shown properly in black-and-white photography. Words can do only so much; they can convey uses and concepts, but they can never do what color can.

In such situations go for four colors. It really would not pay to go without it. And you don't have to pay all that much to go with it.

Four-Color Bargains

There are specialized printers throughout the country who do four-color printing at almost two-color prices. There must be a catch or two—and there are. But you can probably live with them.

These printers can offer the lower prices because they wait to "gang" a batch of orders and then run them all together on one huge press. That means you get the economy of splitting the cost of a four-color press run with a bunch of other guys.

It's sort of like a charter airplane flight: You cut your expense by sharing the facility but must give up certain luxuries.

Like time. You have to wait until the printer accumulates enough jobs to fill his press, so your delivery time can be anywhere from four to eight weeks. Which means if you have an imminent firm deadline, forget it. Try next time when you can plan far ahead and can be elastic about delivery dates.

Like perfect color-matching. Since the printer is trying to please everybody on the press, he cannot give you the custom service of adjusting his ink mixtures to give you exact color. The orange may be a little redder than you'd like, or a bit more yellow. The red may have a slightly purple tinge that is not entirely accurate. They do try to please everyone, and the results are usually pretty fair. It's still four-color and looks beautiful. If your entire promotion is contingent upon depicting true colors, this method may not be for you. Examples: when you are introducing a new hue of blue fabric and a shade off can kill it; or you are showing a line of imported foods where a slight green cast to the pâté can look like you are selling salmonella. In other words, if absolutely faithful color is vital, skip this printing method. You are better off saving your pennies for a custom run or going to black-and-white photography.

Like quantity. They usually have preset quantity breakdowns; 2,500, 5,000, 10,000, and 25,000 are the standard. It usually isn't too difficult to go along with this stipulation; you can usually adjust your needs to the closest prescribed quantity.

Like size. As a rule, 8-in. × 10-in. and 3-in. × 5-in. postcards are the only sizes available. If you need anything larger; you're on your own.

These may sound like an inordinate number of limitations, but they're fairly minor restrictions that should not be hard to live with. If you need four-color and cannot afford it any other way, it's well worth the compromises. It won't look like a *National Geographic* cover, but it will sell.

Three Colors for the Price of Two

There's one basic difference between the big-budget advertising field and the small-budget advertising field: They spend all their time devising clever ways to spend money, and we spend all our time figuring ingenious ways to save it.

Consequently, we learn to investigate and observe every process involved in the services we purchase so that we can take full advantage of every potential they offer. That's how this three-color-for-the-price-of-two came about.

Printing charges are determined by many factors: size, paper, quantity, and number of colors used. Each color requires a run through the press. So the more colors, the more runs, the more money.

"But isn't each side of the sheet run separately?" we asked the printer. "Why not change the ink when you change the sides? In other words, print black with red on the front, and then change to black with green on the back." He couldn't see a reason in the world why this couldn't be done, except that he'd have to wash the red ink from the press before the switch to green. But since the charge for a press wash-up is only $35, that was no big deal.

As a result, we came out with a folder that was three colors, at a price just a bit higher than for two! It's a technique that offers a wide versatility of design possibilities, and we have been using it ever since. Try it.

Two-Color Effect for One-Color Price

Do you know why the Chinese are reputed to have become the greatest cooks in the world? Because for centuries they were so bone poor that they had to seek creative, versatile ways to cook with what minimal resources they had.

This may be an apocryphal answer, but it makes a handy illustration of how limited budgets lead to endless creativity. Color printing on color stock is another example.

You know about black ink on white paper; that's rock bottom on the printing price scale but how about blue ink on tan paper, or green ink on grey, or maroon ink on blue, or brown ink on tan?

DIRECT MAIL

It's amazing how many color effects can be achieved with just the two elements of one color ink and one color paper. Black is usually the preferred color ink for printing halftones (photographs), since it has the proper strength for bringing out detail. But a dark-color ink, with a density that approaches that of black, can often produce a highly acceptable halftone. Look at the variations you can create.

This is particularly important when you are turning out a newsletter or bulletin of any sort that is distributed monthly. It can get pretty boring in straight black-and-white, and after a while your mailings will be getting a "ho-hum" welcome that means instant wastebasket.

So doodle around with papers and inks, and see what interesting combinations you come up with. You can make each month's mailing look totally different and still pay for only one-color printing!

PLAY WITH PAPER

Paper—or stock, as it's referred to in printing—comes in a tremendous variety of colors, weights, and finishes.

Printers often buy odd lots of unusual papers or have some around from overruns on jobs. Chances are you can get these distinctive papers at regular prices under these circumstances.

Ask your printer what sorts of outstanding or different stock he has on hand. You can achieve some stunning effects that way at no higher cost.

GRAB HIM BY THE EGO

No one can resist a test of his mental ability. Secretly (or not so secretly, as the case may be) every man believes that he is smarter than the men running the country. He is probably right.

Attach a quiz to your direct mail, and the response will floor you. It's a delightfully sneaky way to lure recipients into reading your material.

You can use a standard puzzle, the professionally prepared jobs that you find in books. Or create a test-yourself quiz: "Biz Quiz. Test your reading ability and powers of observation." Now what living, breathing, egotistical human being could resist that challenge? Then give them a rating system so they can reward themselves with the exhilarating proof of their superior brain power: "Give yourself 20 points for each correct answer: 80–above average; 90–extraordinary; 100–genius."

The beautiful part is that if you base the questions on the facts covered in your direct-mail material, you will be forcing them to read everything carefully. What greater prize could you ask for?

We once offered a prize for the right quiz answers in a mailer and drew a response that nearly paralyzed the shipping room. Again it was that old appeal-to-the-ego gambit, only this enabled them to show off their success to their children:

"Here's a little gift for you, son."

"Gosh, Dad, where did you get it?"

"Oh, I won it in a quiz."

The answers we sought were based on finding ten mistakes that had been deliberately hidden among the paragraphs of product prose. Anyone who found at least five errors was awarded a Halloween mask for his kids. The results were phenomenal, and we discovered ten more mistakes that were not intentional!

REPETITION—PULL THE COLOR SWITCH

By the time a direct-mail piece goes out, chances are you are sick of it. After all, you've worked on it and seen it so often that you never want to look at it again.

However, the people on your mailing list have seen it only once (if you're lucky). What's to stop you from reprinting the piece at a later date and mailing it again, and maybe even a third time?

Change the colors, and it will look like an entirely different piece. That's a trick that can save you a fortune. You will be able to amortize the basic expenditure of art and copy. Printing is cheaper, too, because printing negatives already exist.

Different colors, maybe different paper, and even you might not recognize it. This is a wonderful way to stretch your ad budget.

NEWSLETTERS—THE PERSONAL TOUCH

They're great, and everyone reading this book should have one. Now that's a pretty sweeping statement, but newsletters are a low-cost way to create big results. They are uniquely personal and allow a company to establish an intimacy with the customer that cannot be achieved with any other medium.

In the last few years, there has been a proliferation of newsletters—especially from the giant companies that strive to create a just-plain-folks feeling in the market, and, incidentally, to soften harsh news. For instance, I have a cozy newsletter from our telephone company. Nested among the recipes, cartoons, and similar tidbits is a small item "New Rate Increases."

For small companies and especially retail stores, newsletters build up a relationship with customers and prospects that is invaluable.

DIRECT MAIL

A newsletter is a great device for speaking about the unspeakable—those generalities about corporate excellence, good service, better-quality merchandise that are impossible to say outright without sounding like the president's mother.

Everyone boils at the competitor who knocks off a product, manufactures it in his garage, and then peddles it at cut prices. That's the toughest thing to fight in business. You don't want to give him the promotional boost of making a big public statement about the dangers of dealing with Shady Sam, nor does it warrant the expense of a mailing. Then how can you warn your customers of the hazards of buying cut-quality merchandise? That's where the newsletter comes in.

Slipped in among all the newsy tidbits can be a note about the risks of buying bargains, maybe a case history of some disaster that resulted from someone in the industry buying from shady, shoddy suppliers. No names, please—just subtle hints.

Maybe you have a specialized product or service that appeals to a limited market. It is not worth a full-scale mailing, but you want your customers to know it exists. You can feature it in the pages of the newsletter.

Perhaps you have some "slow movers" that you hate to drop from the line; they are profitable, and people do ask for them from time to time. You can show them in the pages of the newsletter.

You have a shipping problem; customers are returning merchandise without asking permission, and you are getting stuck with a lot of unwanted, unsaleable items. Mention the difficulty in the newsletter.

Just think of all the things you would like to tell your customers; censor some of them, and put the rest into your newsletter.

It's also a great way to solicit business subtly. Send a regular mailing to a list of prospects. It keeps your name before them, helps your image (if they enjoy the publication), and reminds them to call upon you next time they need whatever it is you sell.

The newsletter, in effect, is a little newspaper in which you are the sole advertiser. Its primary aim is to build readership, to be entertaining and of value to the reader.

Create a name, usually some sort of play on your company name, have a masthead designed, and plan to mail on a fairly regular basis, possibly every 45 days. It should become something the people on your mailing list becomes familiar with and, hopefully, look forward to.

Now the contents. Current news stories or government edicts that are of interest to the group of readers you are mailing to, with some suitable comment from you. Little anecdotes or jokes are a particularly good idea and assure an extended, maybe permanent life for your paper. Most people have a poor memory for jokes and tend to hold on to publications that contain them.

Create standard features, too, like "Charlie's Corner" with a message from the president of the company. People like to know who's running things. How about a "Great Sale of the Month" story or, if you are a manufacturer or distributor, a "Dealer of the Month" story? Everyone will vie to have his success story and picture featured in print. For a store, wouldn't customers find it interesting to read anecdotes about how someone has made creative and interesting use of the products sold?

Now the commercials. Sprinkled casually through the pages can be your propaganda—casual plugs for your products or services. Don't hit them over the head with these messages, though; weave them gently and introduce them pertinently among the other material. The effect is subtle and stronger.

Here are some examples of how you can lead into these messages.

Caution about Cut-priced Competition

A dinner guest at Groucho Marx's house was very puzzled when he examined the sausage put on his plate.

"But this is queer," he said. "One end is bread crumbs!"

"That's right," said Groucho. "In times like these, nobody can make both ends meat!"

* * *

It's commendable to cut corners in the kitchen, but it's downright dishonest to do so in business. Unfortunately, a few not-so-scrupulous manufacturers in the field are doing just that by selling off-weight packages.

This may not be the most hilarious of jokes, but it does smooth the way to an attack on your competition.

Keeping Your Corporate Promises

A ten-year-old boy had a bad habit of swearing. To cure him, his father offered to get him a pet rabbit if he promised to stop swearing. The youngster kept his promise faithfully, and after a month his father brought him a rabbit. Excited with his new pet, he picked her up, and at that exact moment the rabbit proceeded to give birth to an enormous litter. The boy dropped the mother rabbit in horror and cried: "Son of a bitch! The damn thing is falling apart!"

* * *

Some promises are pretty tough to keep. But we made a promise when we started in business 30 years ago to make only the highest-quality products. And we have never broken that promise.

These are just some ways to illustrate how the light touch can enable you to make some pretty heavy statements.

The newsletter must look like an appealing, easy-to-read newspaper: The size could be anything from 5 in. × 8 in. up to 18 in. × 24 in. It should be one-color ink on white or colored paper. It should have a standard format. Familiarity is important, and maintaining a consistent format builds recognition.

And very important: Liven up the pages with illustrations—photographs of people, products, places, cartoons, or drawings. Art breaks up the pattern of words.

Where can you get this art? Get yourself a booklet of stock art. This is a collection of all kinds of ready-to-use cartoons and drawings in every category. Men, women, children, holidays, occupations, and dozens of others. These are all ready to cut out, paste in, and print from. (Harry Volk Studio, Pleasantville, New Jersey, has a good collection.)

BUSINESS-REPLY CARDS—NEVER LEAVE HOME WITHOUT THEM

Never send out any direct mailing without a response mechanism. The purpose of the mailing has been to encourage the reader to *act now*. You have devised an envelope to induce him to *open* your mailing, and you have been deucedly clever and persuasive in your mailing piece to cajole him into *reading* it. Now you must give him the means to *act* upon the entire effort. Always include a postpaid business-reply card on which the merchandise or service described can be ordered. If you want the recipient to enclose a check, include a business-reply envelope rather than a card. These reply devices must carry a postpaid mailing permit so that the prospect does not have to affix his own stamp, which inevitably acts as a deterrent to ordering. Go to your local post office and get a First-Class Business-Reply Permit if you do not already have one.

A new client recently told me that he did not need a business-reply card in his mailing because "our customers phone in their orders." I insisted and he yielded. The first business-reply card that came back contained an order large enough to pay for the entire mailing. There is a seductive quality about getting a postage-free order card that most people cannot resist. And by including the card, you make it easy for them to order—and isn't that the name of the game?

PUBLIC RELATIONS 8

How to write a news release

They used to call them press agents or publicity agents. If you remember the 1940's movies, you'll recognize the type: brash, glib, cocky, and not too couth, ready to pull any stunt to make the papers—fly to Greenland to sell refrigerators to the Eskimos or to India to offer soap flakes to the women washing dhotis in the Ganges.

"I don't care what you say about my client, as long as you spell his name right!"

Then, somewhere along the way, they turned respectable, got religion. Now they're college-trained in communications; they speak softly and write forcefully. The publicity trade has become the estimable profession called public relations—a most powerful force in government, industry, and education.

Today, when you say public relations—or P.R., as it's commonly referred to—you can mean anything from new-product releases to handling lobby campaigns in Washington; in short, any area of communications that can reflect on the public image of the corporation.

P.R. SERVES THE MEDIA

A good part of every newspaper and magazine you read is composed of information received from public-relations writers. There's no illicit dealing, no subterfuge. It is based on a mutually beneficial relationship between the editors and the P.R. people.

An editor or columnist depends on this information. Years ago, when industry was concentrated in a few urban areas, the writer used to do his own legwork and spadework. Today industry has sprawled into remote hamlets throughout the country and now produces thousands of technologically newsworthy developments every month. It would be virtually impossible for a writer to cover all those beats. So he must depend on reports that come in to him from the companies themselves and their P.R. representatives.

The term "depend on" means just that. Since the editor cannot check on the accuracy of every news release that comes across his desk, he must rely on the absolute veracity of his sources. This is why P.R. people will speak confidently about their editorial "contacts." There is no mystique involved in developing these relationships; all you have to do is prove to the editors that they can depend on you for honest, factual, well-written news stories, and they will happily accept your news releases. You are, in effect, making their jobs easier, and who doesn't look for that?

Once you know how to prepare and produce a well-organized professional news release—and it isn't difficult—you can issue them to the media as new developments occur, and you will soon develop your own editorial contacts.

HOW TO PREPARE A NEWS RELEASE

Suppose a wicked king ordered you executed but permitted you a last-minute plea for your life, providing your presentation was interesting and entertaining. But as soon as you lost his attention, you lost your head.

You would pour out all your vital facts and most convincing arguments fast, right? You wouldn't save any goodies for later, because there might not *be* a later.

That's just the way you must think when writing a news release. The editor had better know the major points of your story immediately, or you'll lose your audience; ramble, and he'll stop reading. A properly written news release, just like a newspaper story, has all the salient points up front. The substantive facts, the descriptive detailing, the minor points, come along later.

You are fighting a battle to capture his interest and hold it. The moment you become impalpable and imprecise, the second you go into hyperbole and overstatement, you've lost.

Who, What, When, Where, Why and How

The prime rule in journalism is that the opening paragraph of a news article must contain the answers to these six questions: Who? What?

When? Where? Why? and How? The assumption is that the reader may never get past that first paragraph, and you want to be sure that he gets all the facts before he takes off.

This is exactly how you must set up your news releases. Bear in mind that the editor will have to convert your release into a news article. Contrary to popular conception, editors are human and endowed with the same qualities of sloth as the rest of us mortals. The less rewrite work you give an editor and the closer you adhere to proper journalistic form, the greater your chances that he'll use your material intact.

Make It News—Not Advertising

No one is kidding anyone else. The editor knows you have prepared the P.R. story for the benefit of your company, but he will print it if the news offers benefit to his readers, if it contains straight facts and no unsubstantiated allegations.

He will not include any advertising adjectives or any statements to the effect that yours is the greatest or any claims that put him in the position of endorsing your company.

You must consider your story as a news article, slanted from the point of view of the readers—what it does for them and how it does it. Skip the superlatives; they'll only get slashed or if too overdone, may get the whole story scratched.

The release should be neatly typed, double-spaced, on company letterhead. The words "For Immediate Release" should appear in the upper right-hand corner. This tells the editor that the news is ready to break now. If the happening-date will be sometime hence, say so: "For Release on June 15."

Whatever you do, never misrepresent facts or timing. If you advise an editor that your product or service offers specific features and will be available for sale on a specified date, it damned well better be so, or you'll be on his blacklist forever.

Every editor worth his salt guards his reputation for accuracy with an intimidating ferocity, and well he should. His integrity is his livelihood. If he tells his readers that something is, and then it isn't, then he soon isn't, either.

He may want to check certain details or ask some questions or want some further elaboration on the facts you have provided. Let him know whom to contact, and make it easy by putting your name and phone number at the top of the release.

> **news from**
>
> C/D SMITH, ADVERTISING, INC.
> Kirby Lane, Rye, N.Y. 10580
> 914/976-7173
>
> contact: Cynthia S. Smith
>
> ACCURATE DATA SYSTEMS, Inc.
>
> FOR IMMEDIATE RELEASE
>
> FREE COMPUTER-BUYING GUIDE ON "HOW TO
> CHOOSE THE RIGHT COMPUTER SUPPLIER FOR YOU."
>
> Tips on how to help you select a computer supplier are given in a brochure called "THE COMPUTER-BUYING GUIDE," which is offered free by Accurate Data Systems, Inc., One Fulton Avenue, Hempstead, NY 11550.
>
> The booklet answers questions such as "What should your computer vendor provide?" and "What is the right size company for me?" It outlines how you should evaluate the proposals and presentations and promises made by computer suppliers who pitch for your business. The guide also advises what questions to ask them and what to look out for when making that all-important final choice.

The Properly Professional News Release: Just take your own letterhead and add the words "News From" right across the top. "For Immediate Release" appears first to inform the editors that the event being described has already occurred. If the happening is yet to come, specify the date "For Release on _____." Note the double spacing and wide margins to allow room for the journalist's own notations when forwarding it to his composing room.

Pictures Speak Louder

Always send a photograph with your release if at all possible. It provides more interest to the story and gets you more space in the media.

If it's a product shot, a picture of new packaging, or a new display, you want a simple, vertical shot—no arty lighting—just good sharp, contrasty, nuts-and-bolts stuff. The vertical shot seems to fit in better with the editorial makeup of special columns in magazines. For instance, the new-products sections of almost every magazine accept only vertical shots.

Here is a special money-saving tip: Send 5-in. × 7-in. photo prints with your publicity releases; it can cut your photo print expense and reduce mailing costs considerably. When you get your 8-in. × 10-in. original photograph from the photographer, send it to a photocopying company and have them make a 5-in. × 7-in. copy negative, from which they will make as many 5-in. × 7-in. copy prints as you need. There's no need to send out the larger 8-in. × 10-in. prints; the 5-in. × 7-in. is just as effective and is completely acceptable by all publications.

When mailing photos, don't forget to insert a cardboard stiffener in the envelope. One crease or crack, and your picture is unusable, and if you've ever seen the manner in which the post office handles mail, you realize that photographs need all the protection they can get.

WHAT SHOULD BE PUBLICIZED

There are some trade magazines that will happily publish the hot story that your truck bays have been repainted. Either they are so pressed for news to fill their pages that they will print anything remotely resembling news or they are so hard up for revenue that they will print any item that might flatter you enough to induce you to toss some advertising dollars their way.

The better publications have specific standards for newsworthy material. Here are the most popular types of stories that are considered acceptable by all media.

The New (or Improved) Product or Service

Every magazine has a new-products section, and it's usually the first and best-read part of the book. When you have a new product or service or have added some improvements or innovations to an old one, that warrants a story.

PUBLIC RELATIONS

NEW RADO FLORENCE FEATURES "FLOATING CRYSTAL"
A new watch featuring a scratchproof sapphire crystal that seems to float on the wrist because of the total absence of a frame has been introduced by Rado Watch Company, Inc., New York, N.Y.

Notice that the main point is in the heading with the word "new" prominent, and that the factors that make it new and newsworthy are completely covered in the opening line. Then follow up with all the details of construction, styling and price.

The Grand Opening

A new plant, new wing, new store, new office, new branch, even refurbished quarters, can be developed into a newsworthy event with a little color and style. Make a big-deal occasion of it. Hire a photographer, set a date, and invite some V.I.P.'s. Local officials are the first choice. They're easy; just tell them a photographer will be there, and they'll show up beaming bonhomie.

If you are a distributor or a retailer, invite executives of supplier organizations. The more V.I.P.'s you have, the more space a magazine will give your story.

You might spring for some liquor and nibbles and then invite the trade-magazine editorial staffs. The press is renowned for their inability to resist a freebie blast, and you usually end up with good coverage and much goodwill that can pay dividends in future P.R. acceptances. After the festivities are over, you will have the basis of an excellent news release. It might run something like this:

VIE & VIN LTD. OPENS NEW WAREHOUSE
Vie & Vin Ltd., Englewood, New Jersey, importers of French wines, celebrated the opening of their new warehouse on June 27, attended by the mayor of Englewood and members of the French consulate. The new warehouse will streamline and extend production facilities to an estimated doubling of capability.

Etc., etc.

You would then complete the release with details of who was there and what future growth and successes the new facility will achieve.

The accompanying photo should show all the company principals, plus as many dignitaries as you can fit in. If your photographer knows his stuff, he will be sure to pose everyone holding identifiable samples of the company products, preferably against a background that shows the company name. When you send out the photos, be sure you attach a caption properly identifying the persons shown.

A New Display or New Packaging

You have repackaged your line or have created a new store display. This warrants publicity. Treat it much as you would a new-product story, and include a photograph, of course.

Packaging magazines are particularly receptive to publicity on interesting packages and displays. If your new design has any innovative aspects or is graphically impressive, send the release to the packaging media as well as to your usual trade publications.

A New Executive, a New Distributor, a Corporate Promotion

Here you want a straightforward story that should be accompanied by a recent portrait of the individual. (Don't send a ten-year-old picture, much as the fellow concerned favors the more flattering rendition. When he gets around to the customers, they're likely to think his few months on the job have aged him rapidly.)

The release should include who he is, what he will be doing, what he is expected to accomplish (here's where you slip in the corporate commercial about specific areas of sales activities), and details of his education, experience, and family. Don't forget the local newspapers. The business pages of the newspapers in the town where he lives and the city where the company is located will gladly include the item.

A New Advertising/Promotion Campaign

An unusual advertising and sales-promotion campaign affords two opportunities for publicity—before and after.

A preview-of-the-campaign release would cover the elements, plans, and projected media scheduled for the program. You could photograph some of the components and collateral material and send it with the release.

An aftermath story would be concerned with the great successes achieved and any specific sales results or human-interest ramifications.

For example, Redactron Corporation, which made word processors, ran a "Free the Secretary" campaign that was aimed at the bright secretaries who bridle at the boredom of incessant typing and retyping. Centered around an ad headed, "The Death of the Dead-End Secretary," which ran in *Ms.*, *New York*, *New Woman*, and *The Secretary* magazines, it offered buttons, streamers, and memo pads saying "Free the Secretary," pointing up how the word processor could take over the drudgery of repetitive typing and free the secretary for more challenging chores.

The campaign struck a contemporary nerve and generated an outpouring of interested correspondence from secretaries and executives throughout the country. The reaction was so intense and enthusiastic that it became the basis of a success-story publicity release that was printed by all pertinent media. This kind of story is of interest to the advertising and sales-promotion publications, as well as to the advertising columns of many newspapers.

A New Catalog

Most magazines have a column devoted to the description of new literature available to their readers. If you have any new booklet, pamphlet, or catalog that would be of interest to the readers of specific publications and, more importantly, whose interest could be of benefit to you, shoot out a release on it. Include a description of its aims, contents, and potential value to the readers, and if it is sufficiently prepossessing, send a photo of it.

HOW TO USE P.R. TO OPEN NEW MARKETS

Sometimes the most way-out outlets for products turn out to be fantastically fruitful. The problem is: How do you uncover these hidden sales sources easily and inexpensively?

Answer: With a little imagination, P.R., and a *Bacon's Publicity Checker*.

Just as the guidebook of the advertising-media departments is *Standard Rate & Data*, the indispensable reference guide of the public-relations departments is *Bacon's Publicity Checker*, available from H. R. Bacon and Company, 14 South Michigan Avenue, Chicago, Illinois 60604. This handy little volume lists every magazine and periodical in the United States and Canada according to category. It furnishes names, addresses, and other important information involving the selectivity of acceptable material.

Go through *Bacon's,* and look for potential sales areas for your products. You will come across markets you never dreamed existed. Be daring. Send new-product releases to the publications of every possible market that could remotely be interested. You may get responses from totally unexpected areas and open up brand-new sales outlets never before tapped.

Be imaginative. Be intrepid. After all, how much will the whole fishing expedition cost? With P.R. you can afford to indulge in the most exotic marketing exploration sorties. Who knows, you may uncover a million-dollar market that had been totally overlooked!

HOW TO MAKE NEWS WHEN NOTHING IS HAPPENING

A good P.R. firm doesn't hang around waiting for exciting developments—they make them. In fact, if you should retain a P.R. organization and then find that they're calling constantly to ask what's new, fire them. They're not doing their job.

You can produce newsworthy articles in many ways. Here are just a few suggestions.

The Prediction

One of the simplest bases for a non-happening news release is the prediction from the president of the company. This is the standard headline-grabbing technique of clothing designers. Remember the chap who hit all the media with the prediction that within five years women would be wearing topless bathing suits?

We picked up considerable linage in newspapers throughout the country with a release that read, "A Soda Fountain in Every Home?" and predicted that homes of the future would have built-in soda systems. Of course, the quoted individual was described as the president of such-and-such a company—and there's the commercial plug.

This sort of approach takes some ingenuity and imagination, but think about it.

Suppose you ran an employment agency. You could issue a story headed, "Hiring by computers seen in 1988," and go on into a statement by the president of the agency foretelling the existence of a city-wide central employment computer bank that listed every job and available applicant.

Numbers, percentages—editors dearly love them. Make a prediction of a specific increased figure carrying specific numbers and it gives an authenticity and substance to the story. As an example, when a client who owns a chain of recreational vehicle campgrounds in Florida started to turn their properties into co-ops, I thought it made an interesting "trend" story (another word dearly beloved by the press). The story I sent to the wire service was headed, "Within Five Years, 89 Percent of the U.S. Campgrounds Will Be Co-ops," quoting the president of our client company. They picked it up—after sending a reporter to further interview our client and other campground owners to substantiate the trend—and we got coverage all over the country. As for the prediction figure, take an educated guess. Make it reasonable and possibly attainable. After all, this is not an exact science.

These are just some suggestions, but as you can see, it's not too difficult to come up with newsworthy predictions. The secret of the technique is to make a statement that is intriguing, maybe even fantastic, but never incredible.

What this technique accomplishes is to endow the quoted person with instant expertise. He has made a publicized prediction; ergo, he is a revered seer. Who wouldn't want to deal with a company headed by such a knowledgeable, respected man?

The State of the Economy

Another device to break into the news media is to have the president of the company come out with a statement about the condition of the economy. It's good, but it may get worse; it's bad, but it will get better. Of course, you must back this up with a few accurate statistics, but these are easily obtained from government agencies, not to mention the daily newspapers.

The Famous User

Nothing gets the consumer more than the sight of a celebrity enjoying your product. You don't have to pay fancy testimonial fees, either. The famous can be surprisingly cooperative—and undemanding.

Keep your ears and eyes open. At some point you will hear of some renowned person who uses your product or service. Write to him with an offer of free merchandise in exchange for permission to photograph him with your product.

Sounds wild, right? After all, with all the money he makes why should he bother with barter? However I've done it a number of times; something for nothing appeals to everyone.

When Yul Brynner was first starring on Broadway in *The King and I*, my secretary excitedly showed me a request from him for a booklet on photo albums offered in our ads. What could I lose? I wrote him and made the barter offer.

Guess what? Two weeks later the photographer and I were backstage at *The King and I*, clicking away at the star—in full costume, no less—obligingly holding our albums. Armed with written permission to use the photographs in our promotion, we left him with about $500 worth of albums (cost: $200).

The Specialized Application

How your product is or can be used, and by whom, can get you space in diversified media you never dreamed of reaching.

For example, you manufacture a lamp. It could be a wonderful piano light. It would be handy on a sewing machine. It's ideal for home needleworkers. It's the perfect light to apply cosmetics by. Philatelists and numismatists (stamp and coin collectors, in plain English) would appreciate its strong direct light.

Here's how you get coverage in music publications, home handicraft publications, stamp and coin publications, women's pages, and beauty-hint columns.

You hire a model for the day. Of course, if you have some particularly photogenic daughters or employees around, they'll do fine. Then find a well-furnished home that has a piano and sewing machine. Some member of the firm is sure to volunteer his place. Nearly everyone is flattered that you rate his home highly enough to want to use it for a photography setting. Then you bring in your photographer, on a daily location rate (usually about a few hundred dollars), and shoot the lamp in use in all possible situations and settings. A smoothly run effort should yield anywhere from twelve to twenty shots.

Then write one basic release that describes the prime construction features of the lamp, its colors, styles, and price, and where available.

Next tailor that one basic release to a series of media with a different heading and opening paragraph, each slanted to appeal to one specific market. For example, the piano picture would go with a release headed, "A Note on Lighting," and be followed by "A new lamp that was especially designed to follow the musician instead of just 'go with' the piano has been introduced by...."

The home handicraft picture might be accompanied with a release that read, "Eye-Light of the Year for Close Work," and then led into an opening paragraph that indicated that the lamp was designed especially for the needs of people who did needlework, crewelwork, and so on.

From that one day's shooting and one basic release you should generate enough P.R. possibilities to get you into dozens of publications. Use your *Bacon's Checker* for the editors' names and addresses—and mail. Then sit back and wait for the clippings and inquiries to come in.

Press Party

This is so important to do, that if you can't find a strong reason to have one, invent it. A press party brings the press and sundry influential people and notables to your establishment and creates a relationship and impression that will accrue to your benefit for years to come.

In public relations, the name of the game is familiarity. If the press knows you, recognizes your name and has confidence in your status and stability, your news releases will be picked out of the pile of incoming mail. Even more important, you will become the expert source for your category. Every journalist keeps a source book of references to be tapped to substantiate or flesh out a story. For instance, if you are a computer software company and the reporter is doing a story on that topic and needs some snappy quotes to give substance and authenticity to his story, he'll phone you. Because you are his handy computer software source, you will find yourself quoted in the press and your reputation will grow.

The procedure of running a press party is fairly simple. I've been to elaborate affairs that run into tens of thousands of dollars. But here's how you can do one that's impressive and effective for under a thousand. The timing is important, both for attendance and cost. I find breakfast parties best because you get people before they go to their offices and get embroiled in the work of the day. Also, the food and drinks served at breakfast is far less elaborate and expensive than luncheon or cocktail parties. If it's a retail store which usually opens at ten, have the party between eight and ten.

Then arrange for product demonstrations. Whatever is new should be shown—and by someone who knows how. If you don't have any attractive, articulate personnel, hire an actor or actress and give them a prepared script. Most communities have little theatres, or college theatrical groups whose members can do the job reasonably and well. Don't *you* do it because you must be free to mingle.

Step 1. Invitations—These should be tasteful folders done by an invitation printer.
   Example
   Mary E. Jones and Robert A. Smith
   cordially invite you to attend
   a hands-on demonstration of
   our capability to provide
   food and fun.
   It's a drinks and breakfast party
   to celebrate our new facility and
   our 10th anniversary.
   June 21, 1984
   9:00 to 11:00 A.M.
   Nassau Plaza
   Hempstead, New York 11550
   516/483-0000
   R.S.V.P.

Note the light-touch wording to make it sound like a party. Also note the promise of liquor—that makes it sound attractive to the press. Include an R.S.V.P. card so that you know well in advance how many people to expect.

Step 2. Mailing List—Send invitations to all members of the local press, including editors of different sections of a single publication (the business editor, the home furnishings editor or sports editor or whatever section would find your products or services newsworthy). Mail to representatives of the trade press if you are a manufacturer or distributor, and don't worry if they are based in different cities. Every magazine has local stringers—free-lancers—who it will send over. Include all the politicos in your area—they'll go anywhere the press appears. Their presence lends importance and lustre to the occasion and impresses the other guests. Invite your bankers and their suppliers; it does their hearts good to see that you are aggressive and out there fighting, and can mean better terms when you need them.

Invite your good customers; they like to feel they made the right decision in dealing with the establishment that attracts such important people. Besides, it fills the hall and that's important; you want the place to look packed and jolly. Be creative with your invitation list, and watch the newspapers. If you notice that an important person is coming to your locality at that time, invite him—what do you have to lose? I know someone who read that the President was planning to be in town to speak at a local event. Just on the off-chance that he might want to show some public identification with the "little people," she got in touch with his advance men. It seemed they were looking for ways to show that our chief executive also was concerned with small business people as well as the Fortune 500 moguls. This was just one of those perfect opportunities. He came, and did get that press coverage.

Step 3. Food and Liquor—Make sure you line up a creative caterer whose work you have seen. It doesn't have to be expensive to be attractive and good. A breakfast party with filled croissants, platters of fruit, quiche, cheeses, danish and coffee, plus large punch bowls filled with Mimosas (champagne and orange juice) and Bloody Marys, make a tasteful spread. Rent glasses and dishes. The cost difference between buying plastic and renting china is minimal but the impression difference is tremendous. As an added touch of class, I suggest hiring two musicians: a cellist and whatever other classical instrument can be transported. The effect of having classical music played by live musicians is stunning and effective. Just find some musicians from local music schools. It's easy and not too expensive, because they are always seeking ways to make a few extra dollars.

Step 4. Last Minute Details—One week before the day, phone everyone who has not responded. Get name tags (the pressure-sensitive kind, but please, not the ones that say, "Hello! My name is . . .") and a guest book. Fill out the name tags as acceptances arrive.

Step 5. Press Kits—These are large folders with inside pockets in which you place company literature, a press release about the event and the company, and any pertinent photographs you have that an editor could use in the accompanying story. Ideally, the kits should have your name outside. If you don't have printed ones, just get blanks and paste your firm's label on the front of each to personalize it. The press likes to take something back to their offices to use as reference material when writing up the event.

The day of the party—Set up someone at the front desk with name tags in alphabetical order. Stack up the press kits here—to be picked up on the way out—and put the guest book here. Then mingle, move around, and make sure the demonstrations are going on steadily.

SUNDRY P.R. SUGGESTIONS

Bacon's and many other P.R. mailing services will handle the whole thing for you. Just give them an original release and photograph, indicate which category of publications you want to hit (use Bacon's numbers), and they'll take care of the rest. They reprint the release and photographs in the desired quantity and mail to whomever you select. It's unbelievably easy—and effective.

Every industry is loaded with trade shows. There are certain fields where there are between 50 and 100 exhibits a year. Sometimes they are small hotel shows put on by a local group, sometimes larger efforts by national organizations. The one thing they all have in common is the need for P.R.

Get a list of all the shows in which your firm plans to participate, and then send off the following letter to the executive director of each:

> Dear Sir:
>
> Can we supply you with exhibitor information, photos, etc., on the XYZ Company's products for this year's show? We'd like to be sure that we are included in the press kit, for example, and would welcome any suggestions you might have.
>
> If this is outside your activities, would you kindly let us know the person or organization handling promotion for the show?

You can achieve a fair amount of success and press coverage with this do-it-yourself method of P.R., but it takes a lot of time and steady commitment to really do the job properly.

If you can afford to retain an outside P.R. firm, do. Good ones are available at rates that range from $500 a month all the way up into the thousands. The rate you arrive at is determined by how intense a coverage you need and what you can afford. Let them give you proposals of what they feel they can do within the restricted guidelines you have stipulated. Don't be "snowed" by a fast talker with glib promises of the cover of *Newsweek*. Ask to see what they have done for others and how long they have been associated with the accounts they handle.

Avoid the "revolving door" operations so prevalent among some large national and internationally operating P.R. firms. The name describes the in-and-out movements of disenchanted clients—usually because of long promises and short shrift. Many of these outfits send in their big guns to secure the account and then turn you over to rank neophytes or itinerant juniors who move around from firm to firm to build impressive resumes.

For a small business with a small budget, your best bet is a small shop where your account is important, and whose principals will give you skilled attention.

RADIO 9

The one-to-one medium

"Should I use radio?" "How can I measure the results of radio?" The answers to these oft-asked questions are "Yes" and "You can't." Radio is a reasonable-cost medium that can be very effective for certain types of products and services. If you have a retail establishment and want to reach people in a specific area, local radio advertising can be a marvellous route. According to recent surveys, people listen to the radio on an average of three and one-half hours a day. In many offices, a specific station (usually one playing innocuous "dentist's office" music) is kept on the PA system all day. It's the one they force you to listen to on the phone while you're fuming on "hold."

Today, you will see radios on many employees' desks. I keep mine tuned to a local station and can't work without it. Then there's the hot "drive time"—usually the most expensive buy on radio. These are the hours during which people are driving to and from work and tune in for traffic information. There's also mothers' car-pool time when women keep the radios playing to drown out the shrieks of their playful passengers and listen for news of how the trains are running so they have some idea when their husbands will be dropping by for dinner.

Print advertising (newspapers and magazines) has its place, but its effect is not total; though you are paying for the full circulation of a publication, your ad may be seen by just a small fraction of the readers. Think about it, do you look at every ad in your newspaper? In a medium where the reader is exposed to groupings of ads side by side with attention-compelling editorial matter, your message has just a 10 percent chance of being seen. But radio is a one-to-one situation. You can't *not* hear a radio commercial, because at that moment the message has no competition for your attention. The cost of radio advertising depends upon your local radio stations' rates, of course, but there are ways to buy bargains.

ROS time is your best possible buy. That stands for "Run of Station" and parallels the newspaper "ROP" (Run of Paper). What it means is that the station runs your commercials whenever they have open time during the day or night, from 5:30 A.M. (or whenever they go on the air) until midnight (or whenever they go off the air.) In other words, whenever they have a free time slot, they slip in your spot.

ROS costs one-third what usual radio rates run, and you can end up with almost the same quality time mix as if you paid top rates. How? By buying at the right time of year! During the slower months, like the first quarter of the year, when most advertisers have retired to lick their fiscal wounds after major Christmas season advertising expenditures, you will find the airways open to you. Since the "hot" time slots are rarely sold out, you will find yourself slipped into drive time and other high-priced hours, but at the low one-third-the-cost ROS rates. Remember that your time position depends solely on the station's supply and demand. Buy when the demand is low, and you'll find yourself enjoying prime time positioning at ghosting-hour rates.

But no matter how ideal the timing of your spots, it won't do a thing unless the message is compelling. Frequently, the radio station has a creative staff who can do a wonderful job of preparing your spots. Now, it's fine to have the owner of the advertised establishment do the pitch, provided he doesn't have the personality of a dead flounder and the diction of a Brooklyn cabdriver. Actually it's very effective to have the proprietor speak to the prospective customers. After all, a retail store is the reflection of the owner; its array of merchandise and total ambiance are based on the taste of this individual so that his personality is important to the customer. But if he does not come across well on radio, then drop the whole idea. Too many times such messages become ego trips for the advertiser who adores being in show biz, and the campaign ends up repelling patronage rather than encouraging it. For instance, there is a commercial for a record shop on my local classical music station that is done by the owner in tones so uncultured that he sounds like he should be pitching pastrami instead of Puccini. If you are the entrepreneur, be honest about your talents and consider relegating the delivery of the commercial to a member of your staff or a professional.

Check with the station for preparation. Most of the time, the cost of production is included in your total time purchase, but that's not worth two cents if the station does not have a competent creative staff. Sit down with the creative director (or reasonable facsimile thereof, depending on the size of the station) and discuss your aims and what you expect the ads to say and achieve. Ask if one of their announcers can do the voice and if the station staff can make the mix of music and sound if needed. Very often the station has a specific policy arrangement with their people regarding charges for their talents. What you are concerned about is avoiding the cost of paying "residuals" to talent—which means giving a royalty every time the spot is aired. Get that cleared up beforehand or you can get a very costly surprise later on.

After your commercial has been made to your satisfaction, stick with it. Whatever you do, don't get "tired of it" before the listening audience has had a chance to let it sink in. On radio, as on television, repetition is the name of the game, so hammer the message home. When you make your time purchase, sign up for a number of weeks with sufficient frequency during each week to ensure hitting the entire audience. As in all media, there is an audience turnover. Not everyone listens at the same time every day. Ideally, you should have your commercial run at least ten times during any week; actually 18 times is the norm.

But don't expect to get a measurable response from radio advertising. You have to buy on the expectation, based on years of other people's experience, that radio contributes powerfully to the cumulative effect of any advertising effort. The best kind of advertising program is an integrated one composed of a mix of media; newspapers, magazines, direct mail, radio, and television, if you can afford it. Each exposure complements and feeds the other. As far as calculating the effectiveness of any advertising, short of going into expensive measurement research, there is no way other than your own awareness of the increase you can see in traffic and sales. If you try to find out which medium brought the customer in, forget it, because they do. I can't tell you how many times we have asked customers where they saw our ads and they name publications in which we never advertised. It is a rare person who remembers exactly where and when he saw the ad that brought him in. Actually his correct recollection would be incorrect for our measurement purposes, because he will mention only the name of the medium in which he last recalled seeing the ad. But what about the earlier exposures that registered in his subconscious until the time he was ready to buy?

Advertising has a cumulative effect. It is a building process that must be constructed over a prolonged period, a continual assault on all the senses of your market, to develop familiarity and desire until that critical moment when the need is immediate and the customer is motivated to make his purchase. Radio can be an important part of this buildup.

VISUAL SALES PRESENTATIONS   10

The invaluable selling tool

If you have ever sold (and everyone has, whether it was a product, a service, an idea, or oneself), have you ever found yourself saying, in the course of the sales pitch, "Now, what I should've mentioned earlier..."?

Have you ever interrupted yourself with a phrase like, "Here's something I want to show you," and then started searching your pockets and attaché case for a letter, a folder, or some other pertinent item, only to find when you finally dug it out that (1) it's slightly crushed and very coffee-stained, and (2) the prospect and you have lost the whole flow of your argument while you were on your little hunt?

Well, this can never happen when you use a visual presentation. All your facts are marshalled in advance, neatly arranged in the correct sequence to lead you straight in getting the order.

A visual presentation is a simplified, illustrated version of your sales story that you show as you give your sales talk. Just like a television commercial, it's a planned combination of words, pictures, and sound that hits the prospect's eye and ear simultaneously, thus convincing him faster, surer.

This modern sales tool has proven so effective that today all large companies equip their sales forces with visuals prepared at great expense by professional sales presentation experts. There is no reason why your sales force should not have the benefit of this same proven sales-building weapon.

This is another area where expensive does not mean more efficient. It's not the elaborate artwork that makes it effective, but the proper analysis and organization of your selling story.

I will show you quite simply how to prepare a visual sales presentation that can, without question, improve the sales performance of every person in your company who uses it.

HOW TO PREPARE A BUDGET-VERSION VISUAL PRESENTATION

You will need the following equipment:

1. An 8½-in. × 11-in. ring binder with plastic sheet protectors. If you can get an easel style, so much the better. The easel has the advantage of standing to give the prospect a better viewing angle.

2. Heavy sheets of white paper (about 12). On these you will paste your illustrations and write your headlines. These will be finished pages of your presentation that will be slipped into plastic sheet protectors of the ring binder.

3. Tissue sheets (about 12) for roughing out the presentation.

4. Soft-tipped pens, in black, red, blue, and any other colors you like. These will be used for writing and decoration.

5. A ruler, a sheet of graph paper, rubber cement.

The actual pasting in is the easiest and last part of your preparation. The first and most important part is planning and arranging it. Here are the seven steps you will follow:

1. Analyze your product or service, and list all the reasons why the prospect should buy.
2. Arrange these reasons in proper order.
3. Make a list of all the points that support and prove each reason.
4. Condense the reasons and proof into headlines and captions.
5. Gather illustrations for your visual presentation.
6. Make a rough page-by-page layout.
7. Paste up and print the actual presentation.

Now let's take these steps one at a time.

1. List all the reasons why the prospect should buy.

Include every possible reason you can think of. You can always cut down later.

For instance, if you sell industrial equipment or components, your list might include: It produces a lot of units; the company has a good reputation and is growing; the product lasts a long time; maintenance is simple; it's easy and inexpensive to install; insurance rates are low; the prospect knows of other plants that are satisfied with the product.

If you sell an item for resale to retailers or wholesalers, your list might include: fast turnover; big demand for this type of product; guaranteed and backed by excellent company reputation; the company's vigorous advertising and sales promotion.

If you sell directly to consumers, you might list: The product offers convenience and comfort; improves health; assures safety; saves money; adds beauty; lends prestige.

If you solicit funds or memberships for organizations, your list might include: past activities of the group; evils they have corrected; improvements they have initiated; how their work has added value to property; who supports their work and who opposes it.

2. Arrange these reasons in proper order.

Put them in order of importance to the prospect so that they build up and lead directly into your asking the prospect to act.

3. Make a list of all the points that support and prove each reason.

Okay, you have a convincing list of reasons to buy, but at this point they're merely statements. Now let's take them up one by one and see what we might say further to prove them.

For instance, if you are selling a piece of equipment, you probably have a heading that says, "It's easy to install." You might elaborate by saying; "It takes only three hours to set up. Unskilled plant labor can do the job. No special wires, ducts, pipes, etc., are needed."

If you sell an item for resale, you probably have a reason to buy that says, "You get a fast sales turnover." Your proof of that statement might be: "Colorful, smart packaging stimulates impulse sales. Low retail price attracts more customers. Heavy advertising campaign presells."

After you have listed facts that prove each of your reasons to buy, your story is pretty well set. Now you're ready to start converting it into a visual sales presentation.

4. Condense the reasons and proof into headlines and captions.

Ever notice the way the headline above every item in your daily newspaper summarizes in "shorthand" what appears in the body of the article? That's what you will do now. It is really quite easy. Going back to the salesman of equipment and his first "reason to buy" that dealt with ease and economy of installation, the headline for that page could be *"Low Installation Costs."* The subheads would be condensed to read:

Quickly Assembled
Plant Labor
No Alterations

For the salesman whose products are sold for resale and whose reasons to buy concern sales turnover, our headline and subheads for that page might read:

Fast Sales Turnover
Eye-stopping Package
Attractively Priced
Presold by Advertising

Your heading should never be too specific, or there will be nothing left for you to say. Just remember that you will be right there to elaborate on each point.

5. Gather illustrations for your visual presentation.

Here's where you decide what you're going to use or make up to illustrate each of your selling points. Look over your reasons to buy, and try to think of what sort of illustration would best emphasize each point.

You can use photographs or drawings cut from your company catalogs, bulletins, or ads. Good sources for appropriate pictures are your trade publications or even general magazines. Just go through them, and you'll get plenty of ideas. For instance, if you want to illustrate that your product has strength, you might clip out a picture of a bulldozer or a strong-looking muscle man. If you want to point up the fact that your product is flame-resistant, you might clip out a picture of a fire from a newspaper, then put a big X through it to illustrate that this cannot happen.

VISUAL SALES PRESENTATIONS

Graphs: Use graphs to show records over a period of time. Growth in sales or markets can easily be shown via graphs that you can make yourself. Cut off as big a piece of graph paper as you need, and make a simple graph using your colored pen to make the curve.

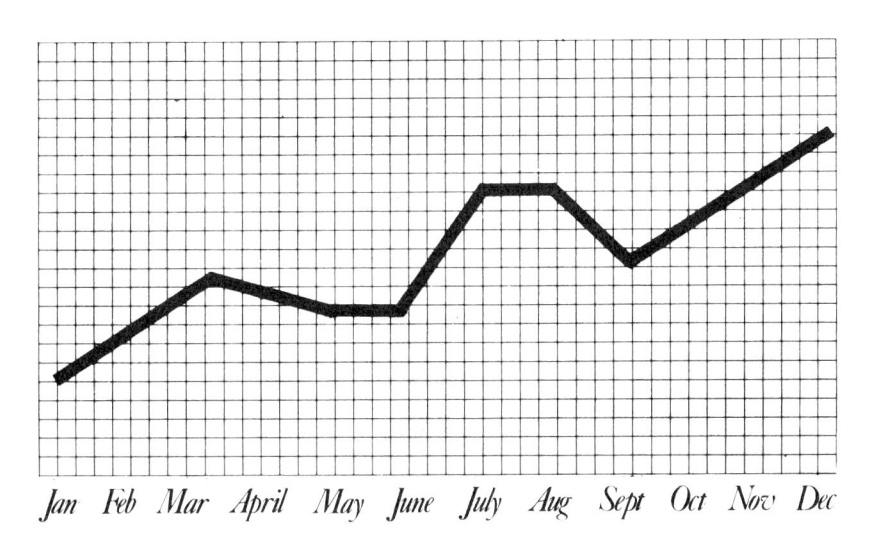

Jan Feb Mar April May June July Aug Sept Oct Nov Dec

Bar charts: Use bar charts to sharpen comparisons between your product or services and competitive ones. You can place the bars vertically or horizontally. Use one color for your product, another for all other makes. Make your own bar charts easily by using thick-nib soft-tip pens or strips of colored tape.

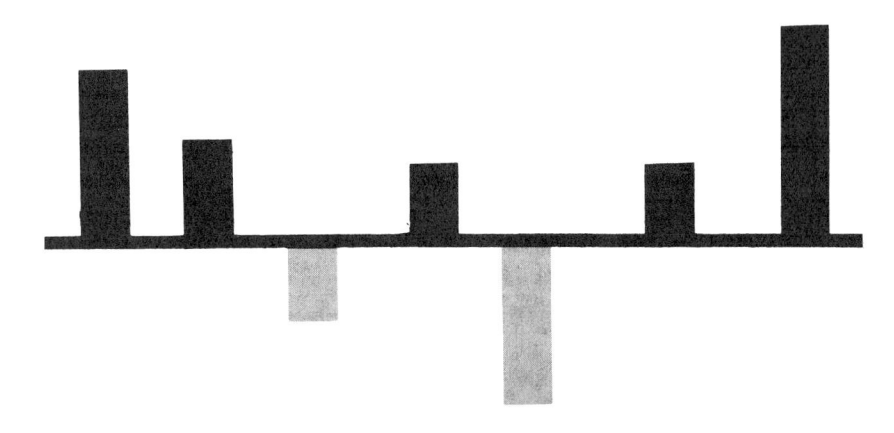

117

Every prospect wants to know which companies thought well enough of your product or services to buy. If a printed list of customers is not available, you can make one by clipping names from their stationery or from ads in magazines. Also, you can get a nice artistic effect by typing names and underscoring them in different colors.

6. Make a rough page-by-page layout.

Now that all your facts are assembled, you're ready to arrange them, or as the commercial artists call it, to lay it out. Use your tissue sheets for this. Take your elements for each page, and rough them into a neat, well-spaced arrangement.

Note: Use only the right-hand pages of your presentation. I never show anything on the facing left-hand page and feature only one "reason to buy" per page. Why? Because it has been proved that if you put one idea on the left-hand page and a different one on the right-hand page, your presentation loses its punch. What happens is, while you're talking about one point, the prospect's eye roams across to a different one, and you've lost his attention. Sometimes, though, if you have a lot to say about one reason to buy you might spread it across two facing pages. Then be sure to run your heading across both pages. But you still permit the prospect to see one reason to buy at a time.

Opening page: This is the page that introduces you and whatever you're selling to the prospect. All it need show is the name of your product plus a picture of it or something representing it. Under the illustration will go a list of all the important reasons to buy. It is sort of a preview of what you will prove to the prospect inside the presentation; it is a teaser to catch his interest. Just write in your headings and subheadings, and merely place your illustrations in position.

Second page: Take your first reason to buy heading, subheads, and ilustrations. For example, you might have a reason to buy plus illustrations like this:

Low Installation Costs	(An actual penny which can be pasted right on the page)
Quickly Assembled	(Your own drawing of a clock indicating, say, a three-hour period)
Plant Labor	(Group of workmen or a man at work, clipped from a magazine)
No Alterations	(Picture of a blueprint with big X drawn through it, indicating that you don't need them.)

Solid, Dependable (Photo of Rock of Gibraltar clipped out of a Prudential Insurance Company advertisement)

Following pages: Take the rest of your reasons to buy, and repeat the procedure. If you have a lot to say and show about one point, make a two-page spread with any two layouts.

Closing page: Here's where you put the all-important sales closer. If you haven't gotten the order before you reach this point, this page gives you the cue to ask for the order now. For instance, you might list the available models of your product here, which prompts you to take out your order book and ask, "Which would be the most convenient for you?" Or you might make this a summary of all the reasons to buy, which gives you the cue to say, "That's why you must buy a ...," and ask for the order.

7. Paste up and print the actual presentation.

Now that you have all your material arranged, you're ready to do the finish on the white sheets. Print all your page headings and all your subheads, but don't let the word "print" scare you. You can use either of two methods to achieve a fine effect. If you are using a typewriter, space the letters out, using all capital letters for main headings and lowercase letters for subheadings, like this:

LOW INSTALLATION COSTS
Quickly Assembled

If you can letter neatly, by all means do your own printing, aided with the ruler edge. Add color by underscoring, circling, or drawing arrows to various headings and sale points. Now paste everything in place on the white mounting sheets, and insert in plastic sheet protectors.

That's it. You now have a well-organized sales presentation that will enable your salesmen to sell more, sell faster, and sell better. Each salesman should have one, but before he uses it, give him the following pointers on how to get the most out of this selling tool.

USING YOUR PRESENTATION EFFECTIVELY

Give the prospect a reason to want to see your visual presentation. Find out about his special interests and problems before you make your call. Then you can get his interest immediately by stating how your product can solve his problems, which leads into your saying, "May I show you how it would work for you?"

STEP-BY-STEP ADVERTISING

For instance, you may have learned that the prospect is having problems with high maintenance on competitive industrial equipment. In that case you could begin your call with, "We have cut down maintenance expenses for ten companies in your industry. This presentation shows how we can do it for you, too. May I show it to you?" In this way he is more receptive—he wants to see your visual.

Know in advance where you will set up your presentation. Pick an advantageous arrangement for showing your presentation. Ask your prospect to clear his desk if that's best. If there are two prospects, try to keep them on the same side as you.

Don't just read your presentation—show interest and enthusiasm. Read the main headline and subheadings, but put sincere belief in your products into your voice.

Use the visual as a stepping-stone to describe details. Here's how you can tailor your visual to each prospect. Read the headline, which is general, then relate it specifically to the prospect. Use appropriate examples of interest to him.

Handle interruptions casually, and get back on the track. Of course, you must answer the prospect's questions. If the point he raises is vital, answer it at once, even if it means flipping to another page. If possible, try to handle his question casually with "We'll get to that in a moment."

Make the prospect part of the story. Wherever possible, try to get your prospect into the act. When you show pictures of companies that have used the product a long time, you might say something like "Their standing in the industry is pretty much the same as yours, isn't it?" When you show the letterheads or names of the companies that have bought your product you could say, "Your company belongs in a fine list like this, don't you think?" Whenever you see that a point has touched a subject close to the prospect's heart, and he wants to expand and elaborate on what you've said, let him take over, and you listen. He'll sell himself a lot faster than you will.

Give life and your personality to the visual. The material in each page of your finished presentation is the skin and bones of your story. It's up to you to give it feeling when using it.

Read the copy printed or typed on the page to the prospect, and then expand the point in your own words. For example, take the opening for a salesman selling industrial equipment. With the presentation open at the opening page, you might say:

"Mr. Jones, I think I can show you how you can save money—lots of money—and really *make* money with our Excelsior machine. You start

VISUAL SALES PRESENTATIONS

enjoying the savings almost from the minute the truck unloads the equipment at your door." Your story stays with him because he has a visual picture of the point you're making before you go on to the next one.

Win the prospect's agreement. Try to get him to nod agreement with the arguments you develop. For example, after you've finished your story on low costs, you might say, "These add up to pretty impressive savings even to a company of your size, don't they, Mr. Jones?"

Ask for the order. Never wait till you get to the end of your presentation to ask for the order if there's an opportunity to do so earlier. If you're selling industrial equipment and your first point impresses the prospect strongly, ask for the order as soon as you've made the point. You could say something like "Our ABC model is just about the right size for your plant. Would you want that, or the CBA model which will take care of some expansion?" If you can get him choosing between models, you've made a sale. If you're selling an item for resale and the prospect responds to a "profit margin" argument, don't wait to finish the presentation to ask for the order. Ask him, then and there, how many he wants for his initial order.

Keep asking for the order right through the presentation. If you get the order at an early stage, close up the presentation, and take out your order book or contract blank. There's no point in continuing the presentation to "sell" him; there might be something in it later on that might possibly "unsell" him.

Of course, if no opening seems to appear as you go through the presentation, make sure you ask for the order after you've finished your story. "Now, which model do you want?" or "How many gross shall we ship you?" or "How much of a contribution can we count on from you?"

Know your story perfectly. Practice the script that goes with each page. Try the presentation on your family, your friends, your associates in the office. Make sure you have the story pat, but don't tell it as though you were doing a recitation. Make sure you know how to answer or take care of every variety of argument or interruption. Then, go out and sell.

Good hunting—and happy closings.

TRADE SHOWS 11

*Bringing in
the buying bodies*

A client of ours had a sales manager. At least, they said they did, and there was an office with the man's name and title on the door. After visiting the company repeatedly over a six-month period and never seeing the man, I began to suspect he was a myth. Until someone told me why he was never there: "He's at shows."

That's one of the dangers of trade shows; you can overdo them.

Years ago, every industry had its big annual show that everyone who was anyone attended. You could be sure that all the important buyers and all the supplier-company brass would be there. Then some smart organizers sniffed the sweet smell of money and started small independent shows all over the place. Then local trade associations decided this was a good way to raise cash and get a piece of the action, and they started small local shows.

Before you knew it, if a sales manager didn't like administration desk work or found his home life a drag, he would—with great show of conscientious sacrifice—manage to involve himself and the company in enough trade shows to keep him on the move ten months a year.

Beware of the "overshow" syndrome, and check the motives and qualifications of any sales manager or executive who insists on personally participating in all of them. A lot of the old-timers of the slap-'em-on-the-back and press-the-flesh school overrate the importance of trade shows. It's usually a substitute for the more modern selling techniques that they cannot grasp.

Many small companies have such men who function as sales managers without really fulfilling or even understanding the full ramifications of the job. Often individuals who started as "outside men" years ago sort of grew into the role of handling sales. They don't really know how to direct a sales force, are totally unfamiliar with scientific sales techniques and motivational methods, and are a severe liability to their companies.

But, getting back to trade shows: I am not deprecating their importance. They have a vital place in business. They can be extremely expensive, what with the costs of the space, attending personnel, transportation, and the display structure. That's why it is important to get the greatest possible value from each show, to develop the most effective display for your needs, and to devise ways to attract the most traffic to your exhibit. There are five basic kinds of displays: crated, self-contained, prefab, stock, and modular.

THE CRATED UNIT

Crated units can be as simple or as elaborate as you like or can afford. They are made of all sorts of materials—wood, plastic, masonite, etc.—and are shipped in a wooden crate (which often costs as much as the display). There's the rub. It's a pain in the neck waiting around at a show to have the crate opened, removed, and brought back when it's time to pack up—not to mention the huge ransom extorted by the assorted union-affiliated gentlemen who are designated to handle it. If you have ever dealt with these gallant chaps, you know that the number of hours you wait for your crate has a direct correlation with the number of bills you pile on their palms. So the crate becomes like a man's hat which must be checked everywhere; it's not the initial cost that gets you, it's the upkeep.

THE SELF-CONTAINED UNIT

Here's how you can avoid the costly crate. The self-contained unit is designed to fold up into itself and become its own shipping container. It is a display on the inside and a crate on the outside.

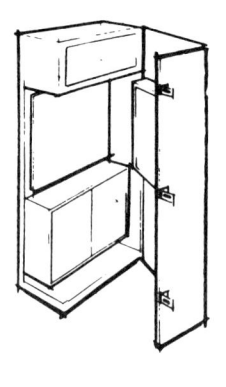

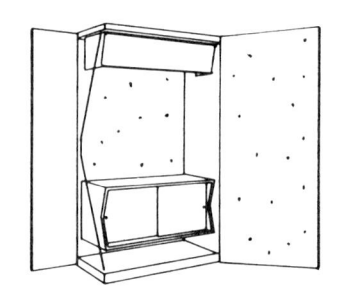

Stock Displays: Design your own exhibit economically and easily by combining stock units to suit your specific needs. The manufacturer will help you assemble sections for special uses, such as one with shelves to hold one style of merchandise, another with pegboard, enabling you to mount samples, and so on. Select the spot lighting you want, have the display sprayed whatever colors you wish, and arrange for your logo to be reproduced on the header sign.

THE PREFAB UNIT

Prefab units are the least expensive displays you can get. They are made of corrugated board that has been merged to pegboard.

This sort of display comes knocked down and must be hooked together in a rather tedious way, but the company you buy it from can arrange to have someone at the exhibit site to help set it up.

STOCK DISPLAYS

Many display houses have stock display units that they will customize for you. They will paint your company identification on the header, add lights where you want, and paint the entire display in your choice of colors.

The stock display can be a very economical solution to the multi-show problem. After all, one display cannot be in more than one place at a time. Sometimes there is an overlap in show dates, with one of the shows being of lesser importance. Here it is a good idea to have a less expensive stock unit that you can use for the minor shows.

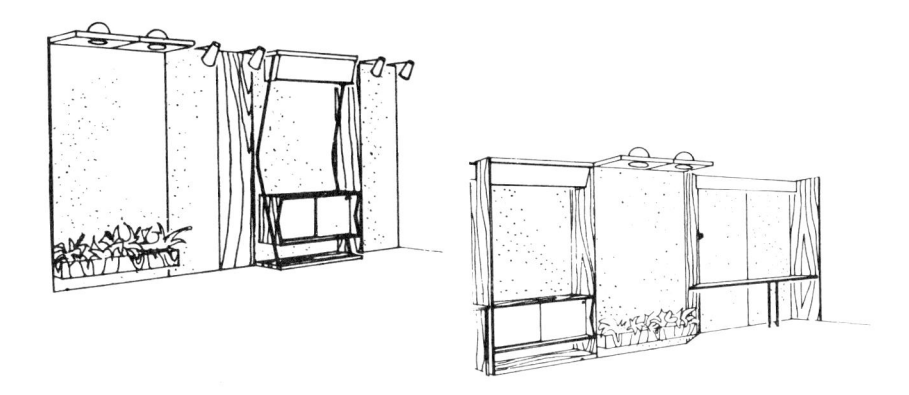

The Self-contained Unit: No shipping case is needed, which means you are saved hours of waiting for the return of your crate when packup time comes around. And you also save the required ransom you must pay to the managers of the exhibit hall if you want to see your crate in your booth before midnight. Note the entire display folds into itself, forming its own crate.

MODULAR DISPLAYS

If you find you must participate in a number of major shows and each one demands a different-sized exhibit, you need a modular display.

Have the display designed in sections so that you can add and subtract sections to accommodate the varied exhibit spaces.

Of course, you, personally, will not design whatever unit you choose; but you will direct the professional display firm that you engage and tell them what specific features you want included.

ISLAND AND COUNTERS

When given a space to furnish, most people tend to push everything against the walls, leaving the entire inside of the room vacant. This sort of uninspired interior decorating shows a lack of understanding of how furniture should be used to form spatial and traffic patterns.

Don't make that mistake when designing your exhibit. Don't cover the back and sides only, leaving a bare hollow in the middle.

Use islands and counters to get more out of the limited space, make your booth more interesting and inviting-looking, and get more efficient traffic patterns.

A center island coming out at right angles from the rear wall is very functional. It divides the booth into two selling areas, so that two salesmen can work simultaneously without falling over each other. This island can be a counter, a bookshelf, or any sort of free-standing unit that serves both sides.

A counter or table or island in front of the display, coming at right angles from the sides of the booth, can be your most effective sales-stimulating area. It furnishes a display space at the prime traffic spot—right where it hits the eyes of passersby coming down the aisles. This is a good spot to set up your new product or announcement of any unusual offering.

It also can perform the invaluable function of inviting potential customers to stop and browse, unhampered by the threat of having to commit themselves to entering the booth.

The hardest thing to accomplish at a show is to lure people in. There are usually so many things to be seen, so many floors to be covered, that visitors are loath to be drawn into any booth other than those of their prime suppliers. You have to do it insidiously, to seduce them subtly, stop them as they pass with a particularly intriguing front-counter presentation. Then, as they linger to examine the offering, your salesman has the chance to make his pitch and, possibly, provide enough incentive to convince the browser to enter the booth.

CARPETING? COUCHES?

Have you ever walked down trade-show aisles and passed booths where sales personnel were lounging comfortably on couches and chairs, maybe chatting happily with each other? I say "passed booths," because that is what you will usually do when you see such a cozy scene. After all, who wants to be the bad guy who breaks up the party?

This is why I discourage the installation of too-comfortable seating in a trade-show booth. I don't mean to be harsh or unsympathetic to the plight of the people who work trade-show booths. I have done it myself many times and am familiar with the attendant rigors: the stretches of deadly boredom when not a soul turns up for hours, alternated with the frenetic bedlam when suddenly 200 people start swarming in groups of tens; and always that persistent, pervasive aroma of greasy hot dogs and burned coffee.

Of course, seating is needed, but it should be purely functional, not the kind that encourages lounging. Too-comfortable salesmen intimidate people and discourage browsing. They are loath to disturb the recliners and will frequently pass by rather than intrude.

Also, a comfortable couch encourages visitors to hang around and rest awhile. Now I'm all for hospitality, especially for customers. But once you've taken their orders, who needs them cluttering up the booth?

Carpeting is a good idea. Feet go fast at a show, and they need all the help they can get. The floors are cold and hard and become more so as time goes on. You can usually rent carpeting, or bring your own. Since we discourage sitting, let's at least make standing more comfortable.

DISTRIBUTE LITERATURE, NOT CATALOGS

"Er-er, have you got a catalog?"

That's one of the most asked idle questions heard at a show and the one that can cost you a fortune in wasted literature.

A person visiting a trade-show booth feels he ought to walk away with something. It gives him a sense of accomplishment, as though he has done the correct businesslike thing. After all, he is attending the show to amass trade information, and here he has amassed some—a catalog. Later, when he has the time—back in his office, or home, or hotel room—he'll look it over and study it carefully.

Uh-huh. Sure he will, if he still has it when he gets there.

On the other hand, maybe he has bothered the salesman and bought nothing. People feel less guilty about walking out when they ask for a catalog, thus leaving the salesman with the hope that there may be business forthcoming.

Perhaps his intentions are strong, but unfortunately his arms get weak. After accumulating catalogs and other literature from booth after booth, lugging the sack of stuff around becomes burdensome. It's tough enough dragging your own body around floor after floor of exhibit area without adding pounds of dead weight. Soon the gleaming relief of a trash can comes into view, and he unloads the whole pile without even a backward glance. Take a look at the wastebaskets at trade shows sometime, if you want to get depressed. They are packed with thousands of dollars' worth of literature.

How to avoid this gross waste? Don't distribute catalogs at a show!

The best technique is to answer the "Do you have a catalog?" gambit with "Surely. We'll be happy to send one to you. May we have your name and address?"

Keep a batch of catalog request cards on hand. The advantage of this method is threefold. First, you know the catalog will reach the buying prospect when he has time to read it and where he has the facilities accessible for sending in orders.

Second, this filling-in-the-card method gives you the golden opportunity to hold the person in the booth while you are writing, and this forces him to look around. If you write slowly enough, he might have the chance to see everything you have, and maybe even become interested enough to buy something on the spot.

Third, you accumulate a list of likely prospects. You do need some literature at a show—throwaway material such as catalog sheets, circulars, or envelope stuffers. Why offer it at all if it will be discarded instantly? Because this material performs the same service as point-of-purchase displays in a store. It supplies the prospect with a product's salient selling features and all the important information that the existing salespeople do not know or the nonexistent salespeople can't give.

Often, when the booth becomes crowded, a customer or browser will pick up a piece of literature and read while awaiting his turn. He can sell himself or pick up facts the booth salespeople may not remember to convey.

Just remember to keep all the literature accessible and neat. Nothing makes a booth look worse than assorted advertising literature littering the counters and floor.

GIVEAWAYS

The most repellent breed of show visitors are the booth-beggars. "Whaddya giving away?" is the usual greeting of this charming bunch. A good kick in their bulging shopping bags is what they deserve—and all you should give them. Anyone who comes into the booth with that "gimme" attitude is not a serious buying prospect and should be ignored.

I am against show-time giveaways: I cannot see where they achieve any benefit for the donor, except to attract a lot of deadbeats who are looking for freebies, antagonize them when they are refused, and waste booth personnel effort in distribution. All in all, a big waste of money.

What's the point of giving gifts to someone who has already found your booth? The aim of every show promotion should be to draw traffic—but selected traffic. A booth that is jammed with the "gimme gang" looks busy, all right, and may cause much envious teeth-gnashing in your competitors' corners, but it produces zero business for you. In fact, prospective purchasers are often deterred by the crowd, so that non-buyers could crowd out the buyers.

TRADE SHOWS

HOW TO PULL SELECTED TRAFFIC

There is a sure method of getting almost everyone on your mailing list to stop by your booth. It's a simple idea—so simple you wonder that it works so well. But it does—fantastically.

All you do is send out a mailing, no later than a month before the show, containing a gift certificate, "redeemable only in person at our booth." Now here's the secret ingredient. The gift *must* be something for a wife or child.

The response will amaze you.

I remember the first time that I used this gift certificate approach, the sales manager predicted that the whole idea would be a surefire fiasco.

"You think any guy will bother to come in for a cheap piece of jewelry?"

You should have seen his face as the steady trek of coupon-bearing buyers began streaming into the booth! He saw buyers who had just been faceless names on our mailing list for years, poeple who had never before visited our exhibit.

They bothered to come, all right, and the psychology is very simple. A man who has been away at a trade show usually returns home with a bit of guilt tucked into his bosom. Maybe he has a valid reason for the guilt, or maybe he's just a nice guy who has had some fun and feels sorry for his wife, who's home with the kids. So he likes to bring home little goodies. Especially a piece of jewelry. It makes him feel like Santa Claus.

Then there's the coupon-signing-in-the-booth gambit. That's a plus for your side, because he must stand there and sign his coupon before redeeming it, and the salesman must rummage around a bit to find the gift. That takes time—calculatedly so—time to allow the buyer to look around, maybe to pick up and idly inspect a product, which is an opening for a smart salesman to say: "That's our best-selling product, and, believe it or not, you picked out the best-selling color!"

Remember, he's psychologically beholden to you—because he is in there asking you for something. If you can sell anything, now's the time!

Now, some advice about the gift. It should be a classic-looking piece that appeals to all ages. And since it must be inexpensive to make mass distribution economically feasible, observe the rule that should be followed whenever buying any budget-priced merchandise: Keep it simple. The less detailing on the piece, the less chance to expose shoddy workmanship.

The most successfully accepted piece I ever used was a pearl-drop pen-

129

dant on a gold chain. Maybe because of the impressive legend on the box, "genuine cultured pearl, 14 kt. gold-filled chain," maybe because of the classic simplicity of the jewelry. A gold heart on a chain is also a popular choice.

And it *must* be nicely boxed. Packaging is a very important way to convey value. Jewelry usually comes in a small cotton-padded gold or white box, which looks very impressive. You can buy this sort of gift item from manufacturers of costume jewelry or from premium houses. Sometimes you can get a special closeout at a very good price. Stuffed animals are great successes, too.

SHOW-TIME HINTS

The next thing you want to do after luring a live prospect into the booth is to crack open that order book. That's sometimes harder than the pulling-in procedure.

It's kind of a game you play. The customer pretends that he really just came by to look, and you pretend you just want to show him what's new. No one likes to mention that dirty word "order." Not right away, that is.

So how do you manage to make the transition from the role of genial host to the one of crassly commercial order-taker? Gently.

That's where a prepared deal comes in—particularly a low-ticket one that includes something new. Here's how the dialogue goes:

Customer: Well, what have you got that's new?

Salesman: Here's our new number 607, a completely new departure, something your customers will flip over.

Customer: Hmm—nice. How much?

Salesman: Only $2.25 retail. Matter of fact, we're introducing it in this show-special deal—an assorted dozen for only $25, but you can only get this if you order it right here. Would you like one?

Customer: Well, okay, might as well.

Once the order book is open, it is up to the salesman to keep writing.

Besides the lower-ticket order opener deal, you should have many other preset "show-special deals" for all of your products. It makes it easier and faster for the salesman to sell, and once he gets the customer going in a buying mood, it's go-for-broke time.

Most show managements grandiosely offer participating exhibitors an unlimited supply of show invitations—imprinted with their specific booth number. They suggest that you send them to your customers to tell them to come in and visit.

Now, why pay the postage of the weight of these cards when you can say the same thing right on your mailing? You can print in a prominent spot, "See us at the —— Show, Booth No. 002," and you've said it all. There is nothing gracious or individual about their invitation cards. You must realize that they are offered to all exhibitors, and chances are that your customer list is receiving the same card from other suppliers. The show management loves it; this is great advertising for them. But what's in it for you?

Second to "Where's the rest room?" the most asked question at a show is "What's new?"

And it's natural. Most exhibitors use shows to introduce their offerings, and most visitors come to find out about the latest innovations in the industry. So make it easy, and make it obvious. They have come to see it, and you have come to sell it.

Put whatever you have that is new—whether it's brand-new or you have added a widget and it's newly improved—up front and in the center with the big, bold designation **"NEW."**

Ever see what a booth looks like after a siege of sales? Each product is strewn where the last man who handled it dropped it, and the place is a shambles. Unless you get the chance to tidy up again before the next wave of customers hits, everyone will be working under the handicap of being unable to find what he is trying to sell. Nothing loses a prospective purchaser's interest faster than waiting for a salesman to burrow through a pile of merchandise to find whatever it is he thinks the customer should buy.

The only way to prevent constant chaos is to have a collection of marked samples mounted permanently to the display. Additional stock can be loosely distributed around the booth. But the salesman can always depend on finding a representative sample of every item whenever he needs it.

SETTING-UP TIME

There's nothing more dispiriting than standing amid a pile of unopened cartons in an un-setup booth, knowing that you have to set it up. There's that helpless feeling of wondering how to begin and where to put what.

If you have some artistic ability or taste and experience, you will probably end up with an attractive-looking arrangement after a few sweat-soaked hours. But if, like most people, you have no ability in these directions, the end result is apt to look pretty grim.

That's why it is a good idea to have someone back in the home office, who has some talent, taste, and time, draw up a diagram—a simple drawing instructing the setting-up personnel just where each piece should go. This simple how-to-set-up-the-booth diagram will save hours of work and aggravation and ensure a tasteful, attractive display.

HOSPITALITY SUITES

There is a feeling in some corners of industry that a free flow of liquor brings a big flow of business. I don't know on what instinct they base that opinion, because the facts surely don't back it up.

At every trade show there are always some "hospitality suites" around. A "hospitality suite," in case you are not familiar with the name, is a couple of hotel rooms taken over by a company, to which buyers are invited to pass the time of day and hoist a few in the name of friendship.

The aim of the "hospitality suite" is to get the buyer into a noncommercial atmosphere and sell him softly in a social ambiance. Maybe this works in a large company that has a rotating group of personnel to run the suite.

However, a small company has a small executive roster and the same crew has to be on duty pretty much of the time. Thus by about two o'clock in the afternoon the hosts are suffering from a severe case of over-hospitality and not really sure what they're selling or to whom. As a result, the image conveyed to buyers is apt to be of a company run by giggling, glassy-eyed executives with upside-down badges. It is not one to inspire confidence.

Also, you run the risk of becoming a second home to the deadbeat drinkers who are found in every industry. If they are customers, you can't throw them out, so you're stuck.

All in all, for my money and yours, a hospitality suite is bad news.

SALES MEETINGS 12

Love 'em and lead 'em

Sometimes when you're facing the sea of sullen salesmen's faces, you wonder what masochistic madness prompted you to call this meeting in the first place.

It's a good question. Because if you've ever had the misfortune to be at a hotel when it was hosting a corporate sales meeting, and you see the sophomoric sybaritic bedlam that passes for pleasure among so-called grown men, you wonder what the company expected to accomplish.

Actually, the sales meeting has a very vital function in a company's sales-building structure. Today too many large corporations use sales meetings as a reward for underpaid salesmen, and the valid basis for the meeting gets buried under a lavish mix of wine, women, wives, minks, and liquor.

Fortunately, since we of the small business world don't have all the cash to cast about, sales meetings must be sales meetings, and they can be very effective.

LOVE AND CATHARSIS FOR SALESMEN

Salesmen want money, but they also need love. They spend their days currying the favor of testy buyers, courting rejection at every turn, trying to be not just liked, but well liked.

STEP-BY-STEP ADVERTISING

They need the ego satisfaction of corporate recognition. They need to know how important they are to the existence and future of the company.

That is one of the prime purposes of a sales meeting. To publicly acknowledge the salesmen's importance. It gives them a shot in the arm, a feeling of affinity with the company. They like to know that while they are out there doing battle among the hostiles, someone up there likes them and truly cares to know what they think, feel, and want.

A meeting is a great catharsis for them and allows them to air all their grievances. That's one of the things you have to watch for, though. Sometimes you get a couple of master gripers together, and the whole meeting can disintegrate into a tirade of complaints and self-pity.

Getting all the salespeople together can be very informative for them as well as for management. They get the important opportunity to exchange ideas, discuss mutual problems, and pass along solutions to one another. Chances are that a knotty situation the salesman in Duluth has now is much the same as what the fellow from Akron handled last month. Each can learn from the other's success or failure.

If you hold the meeting in the company's hometown, take the sales force through the factory to familiarize them with new manufacturing techniques and old production problems. A salesman tends to think in a very insular fashion. His concern is only his customer and his commission. But when he sees the plant situation, he often gets a new overview that helps him to understand why orders cannot always be shipped when and how he wants them.

To customers the salesman *is* the company. His is the face you present to the market, and you want that face to be a happy one. You want it to reflect a secure, solid situation.

The salesman should be 100 percent behind the company and not move over into the customer's corner when some difficulty arises. Sales meetings promote the salesman's feeling of belonging, of being a part of the organization, and help him to identify fully with the company.

PLANNING THE SALES MEETING

If you were laden with a lavish treasury of tax-deductible sales-promotional dollars, you could toy with a choice of exotic sites for meetings, from chartered ships to romantic islands. Since we are working close to the bone, there are only two economical methods of getting the sales force together. You can fly them all in to the company's hometown for a few days (or overnight), or you can wait for the annual trade convention.

Flying them to the company's hometown is the best way, because you have their undivided attention, and you have the various company facilities and personnel available within hailing distance.

However, this can be relatively costly, because you have their air fares and living expenses—and this can get to be a hefty tab. On the other hand, if the budget can bear this, it can be an invaluable experience and an extremely worthwhile investment that will pay dividends all year.

The alternate method—waiting for the annual trade convention—is the economy version. Since all salesmen must attend their industry's annual trade convention, this is one way to get them all together, without having to spring for additional fares.

If they are manufacturers' representatives, they pay their own way to the convention, so you are spared even that. If they are your own men, you would have had to pay for their trips to the convention city, anyway.

How to Pick the Place

Your first step is to reserve a meeting room at a hotel, convention hall, or anywhere that is nearby and convenient.

Be fussy about the place. A shoddy, tacky room with rickety furniture and peeling paint does not convey a successful upward image to salesmen. Be alert to the ambiance—it's important.

Look around at the decor; check into the service. Be sure it's a place that caters to meetings and has the proper facilities. Don't settle for a hotel dining room or suite that becomes an instant meeting room by throwing some green felt over a few tables.

Try to get a sunny, bright room. Cheerful surroundings can add immeasurably to the positive mood of a sales meeting, and the size of the room is vital. Don't get a place that is so huge and cavernous that voices echo and intimacy is lost. Nor should it be so small that everyone is rubbing knees. Select the right size to accommodate your number of participants.

How to Pick the Time

Morning is preferred! Try to make it a breakfast meeting. The morning is a far better time for many reasons. First, everyone is fresh and reasonably alert. Second, the early hour gives you a respectable reason to avoid the alcohol problem.

Liquor has its place in living and business, but it has no place in a sales meeting. I know it's a stimulant and a lovely relaxant, but ever try to talk seriously to overstimulated and overrelaxed salesmen? It can be a total waste of time and money. You can serve all the liquor you want after the meeting is over, but never before or during.

The Agenda

Before you start, be sure a pad and pencil have been placed before each salesman. At the onset of the meeting make a little announcement to the effect that they can use these pads to note down questions they would like to ask each speaker after the entire program is over.

No questions or discussion allowed during the program—and that's an order. I have seen interruptions and questions destroy speakers and even wreck an entire sales meeting. Once a company I was with had based its entire presentation around a new indestructible Mylar-laminated ring binder. That was when DuPont had just introduced Mylar, and it was hot news.

A sample of the Mylar-coated binder was placed in front of each salesman. (Mistake number one. A sample of each new product should be passed around as a speaker is discussing it—never left in front of the salesman throughout the meeting for him to play with.) The company sales manager made an enthusiastic speech about this exciting new book that was going to revolutionize binder sales and knock competition for a loop, because it was virtually untearable and uncrackable. While he talked, the company's number-one crank, a salesman known for his cantankerousness, carefully picked away at the laminate, doing a thorough job of loosening the adhesive. By the time the sales manager was just hitting the pinnacle of his pitch, predicting a rosy economic future for all at the table if they just went out and pushed this superlative new product, Mr. Lovable raised his hand to ask a question: "You said this binder won't tear?" Whereupon he stood up and calmly ripped the cover right down the middle.

Bedlam ensued. No matter how we tried to explain that the binder would never tear with normal usage, that nothing was safe against misuse and vandalism, it was too late. The psychological damage had been done, and the whole presentation shot. Six months of product development, advertising, and sales promotion plans also were gone.

If the salesman had been forced to save his question until the end of the meeting, after the production manager had explained the construction and qualities of the binder, and after other subjects had been covered, the impact of this little bomb would have been lost. And, of course, if he hadn't been given the chance to pick away at the product for an hour, the entire disaster would have been averted.

Some people are devout iconoclasts. They get a perverse pleasure out of tearing down what others build or believe in. These are the sort of inquisitors who can break up a sales meeting with negative thinking and contentious questions. So head 'em off at the pass, and allow no questions or interruptions until all speakers have finished.

SPEAKERS—HOW TO KEEP THE MEETING MOVING

The meeting of a small organization should always be opened with a short talk by the head of the company. The speech is usually intended to be inspirational, although most of them inspire nothing but boredom.

Since you, as the person concerned with communications and sales promotion, will probably write the speech, make it short. There's nothing that deadens a meeting faster than a long-winded, presidential-type rendition of clichés and homilies. Those recollections of past glories so beloved by company founders are guaranteed instant eye-glazers.

Avoid them. All a presidential opening speech should say is: "Glad to see you all here; we've had a great, exciting past, and let's look forward to a great, exciting, profitable future together. We can't miss, when you hear all the great things our people have planned for the coming year, and let's get to it." Put it simply; maybe add a light touch here and there if you can. The sales force will always listen respectfully to the president of the company, but don't make it a punishment.

The sales manager is the person who makes the salesmen feel as if they have hitched their wagons to a star. The sales manager's pitch should be positive, exciting, action-packed, and filled with plans and promises.

What we did last year "you and we together." (Very important! Keep the "I's" out of these speeches. It's "we" or nothing. After all, where would a sales manager be without salesmen to manage?) Then he unveils the plans for the coming year.

A good way to really get the salesmen in the palm of his hand is to personalize his talk. Include a one-by-one comment on each salesman's successful performance in the past. A mention of some specific large sale, some hard-to-crack account he finally won, some public statement of each person's achievement before his peers. The purpose of the sales meeting is to activate the salesmen. There's nothing like a little recognition to motivate a man to perform.

It is very important that the sales force be given a strong positive picture of the company and its future. I don't mean phony promises about riding off into the glowing sunset together. Nor any equivocation about any unpleasant facts and figures. Distortions court disaster.

If the past year has indeed been a poor one, face up to it, and explain the situation honestly. There's no sense trying to hide poor sales figures, because salesmen have an incredibly efficient grapevine. When something happens in the main office, they seem to hear of it almost as fast as the company switchboard operator (a breed whose intelligence-gathering system makes the C.I.A. look like the Boy Scouts). Official denials only add to the salesmen's apprehension.

As long as the ending note is a positive one—with a realistic assessment of the company's potential based on the vigorous new plans—the sales force will be with you. Whatever last year has been, make them feel they are with a progressive, ambitious company and that any setback has been a temporary one. Keep them loyal, enthusiastic, and believing that they have a good solid future with the company.

When the ad manager speaks, he should also delve into past history, giving a little review of last year's successes—"thanks to your cooperation," of course.

Next reveal the new advertising and sales promotion plans for the coming year, and enlist their support, "which we need and depend on." Talk of the future—and the distant future—and of plans that are actually now in the works and blue-sky brainstorms that will be coming along soon.

Now here's the person they have all been waiting for—the production manager. This is "Mr. Unavailable" they can never get to see or talk to in the plant. He's always harried and hassled with labor problems, delivery defections, slow shipments, production and machinery malfunctions.

However, he's the man who knows how the products are produced and why they sometimes do not turn out exactly as the salesmen would like.

Write a short speech for him, *and allow him to deliver it sitting down.* Production managers are usually not too articulate and are often surprisingly panicked at the prospect of public speaking.

I say "surprisingly" because I remember my shock when I saw a production manager whom I was accustomed to hear howling at burly machine-operators, barking profanity-punctuated commands to teamsters, unable to stand before a sales meeting because his knees were trembling! I remember being glad that I had written his speech on cards, because if it had been on paper, the rattle of the shaking sheets would surely have drowned out his words.

I have never been able to quite understand why speaking before a sales meeting terrorizes some people. I could understand it if the audience were composed of total strangers, but sales meetings are attended by people the speakers have talked to and worked with for years. There's rarely an alien in the house. Yet en masse they seem to present a threat that throws many an executive into a tizzy. (The use of visual devices sometimes takes the speaker's mind off his fears.)

The production manager's talk should explain production problems so that the salesmen become more understanding about unfilled manufacturing demands.

Salesmen can be the most unreasonable of creatures. When customers ask for special adaptations or custom-made merchandise, the salesman naturally wants to take the orders, but these demands are not always realistic or feasible. Here's the time to explain why and equip the men with enough knowledge to know when to tell a customer that it cannot be done, rather than waste the time and effort of writing to the company.

Talk of new machines, if any, new production plans, and new techniques that will expedite future production. Then close with thanks for their patience and understanding.

The Question Period

Now the question-and-answer period. If you have done your work right, the salesmen will be happy, the questions will be good-humored, and they will be primed and refreshed, ready to go forth and multiply sales for another year.

THE SECRETS OF SMOOTH SPEECH WRITING

Most executives say that they want to write their own speeches. It's a matter of pride, of course. Actually, they find it an onerous chore and tend to procrastinate. And when it finally does emerge, it is stiff, dull, and disorganized.

So how to write their speeches for them without impinging on their pride?

I have found a method that has worked well and avoids the dangers of damaged dignity and dull discourses.

A few months before the sales meeting, ask all participating executives to please "just jot down some notes" of what they want to cover—subjects they want to talk about in their speeches.

I stress the casual "just dot down" because the sound is less threatening and enables them to unbend and write easily. You can take their notes and "edit them," as you will diplomatically term the procedure, or in plain English, transform them into a speech.

To a nonwriter—that is, someone who does not write for a living—there is something apparently paralyzing about a blank piece of paper. (It's not always an easy thing for a professional writer to face, either.) Tell someone you want him to write a speech, and he will be totally unable to produce a word.

Somehow, people feel that words that go on paper must have a heraldic solemnity. And a "speech"! The very word conjures up images of majestic moving declarations at least as noble as Washington's farewell to his troops. So they ponder, suffer, and sweat, and painfully construct formal, "meaningful" sentences incorporating obscure polysyllabic words they haven't used since freshman English. Ultimately they produce an oration that has the spirit and verve of a last will and testament.

The best way to ensure that your salesmen do not fall asleep is for you to write the speeches.

The secret of writing a good speech is incredibly simple: Make it conversational. Speaking to 50 people is no different than speaking to two; all you do is talk louder.

Use everyday, casual language, replete with contractions and colloquialisms, and they'll listen. Start packing your talk with "show-off syntax"—big words and formal phrases—and a deadly hush soon settles over the audience not because they're spellbound, but because they're asleep.

Organize the speech in three parts: First, state what you intend to accomplish. Second, enumerate how you intend to accomplish it. Last, sum up with a reiteration of the accomplishment.

Visual Aids—The Relaxers

In the theater they call it stage business. It consists of actions and visual devices to keep the audience's eyes from wavering while the performer goes through a particularly long soliloquy.

Have you ever noticed actors' constant preoccupation with cigarettes and liquor? A consistent television watcher would get the idea that fully one-quarter of American adult life is spent finding, lighting, mixing, pouring, and drinking cocktails. Actually, these theatrical preoccupations are merely bits of stage business, activities dictated by the director

SALES MEETINGS

to keep the actors involved in interesting movements while they make some pretty dull conversation. In effect, these are visual aids to keep the audience's attention.

Which is exactly the function of visual aids in sales meetings. After ten minutes of staring at a stationary talking object, eye-glaze time sets in. Thus, it's important that you devise ways to get the speaker to move and to perform some operations of visual interest to the audience. These actions also serve to relax the speaker. As you may know, if you have ever addressed a group, the hardest thing to work out is what to do with your hands, which is why the cigarette-lighting business is so popular. (One of the oldest theatrical cigarette-lighting gambits to ensure prolonged audience attention is to strike a match and just hold it while continuing to talk. After a second the audience's collective eye becomes riveted to that flame, waiting for it to burn down to the smoker's fingers. You can be certain to hold the audience in thrall until the second you blow out the flame, when you can almost hear the sigh of relief.)

Visual devices take the speaker's mind off his stage fright. He has chores to perform and becomes too busy to be nervous.

There are many simple, inexpensive visual-aid devices you can use.

Blackboard—The blackboard is the most oft used accompaniment to speeches because it's easily found and most familiar. However, it is also the least effective.

The technique has the speaker highlight his talk with notes, graphs, and/or diagrams that he writes on the board as he talks—schoolteacher style.

The trouble with the blackboard method is that very few people know how to write on the blackboard. You have to write large; you have to apply the chalk firmly; you have to write clearly and in a straight line. And if you think that's easy, take your mind back to grade-school days when your teacher asked you to come up to the board and work out a problem before the class.

Many people have illegible handwriting on paper but on a blackboard it's even worse.

The other drawback is that it takes too long to write the phrases or figures, during which time the speaker usually has his back to the audience—not a posture recommended to keep attentiveness high.

Magnetic Boards and Easels—These are various types of boards, sometimes called felt boards, that have a magnetic or adhesive quality: You just slap signs on, and they stick.

These boards are available from art-supply and stationery stores, but if you can't find them locally, you can make one easily with Velcro strips.

Velcro strips consist of two pieces of mutually attractive fabric. You merely paste one on your board and the mutually attractive piece in back of your sign, and it adheres on touch. Velcro can be bought in most needlework stores and sewing departments.

The purpose of signboards is merely to punctuate your talk—to point up highlights and build a complete story.

For instance, the ad manager is talking about a planned program of local promotions (as described earlier). To add drama and color to the talk, he would draw attention to the specific areas of attack planned and show the cumulative effect of the total assault by means of signs on the visual board.

The first sign would title the total aim of the campaign: "The Campaign to Capture Cleveland," and as he made the statement, he would slap the sign on top of the board. Subsequent signs, which he would put up to accompany the verbalized point, might say:

"Local Newspaper Ads"
"Dealer Tie-in"
"Cooperative Dealer Advertising"
"Direct Mail"
"Store Window Displays"
"In-store Displays"
"TV, Radio"
"Publicity Tie-ins"

And as the board builds up, the tremendous strength of the impending sales promotional asault becomes visually as well as aurally apparent. It builds to the inescapable conclusion, the sign that reads, "Result: We Capture Cleveland!"

Building Blocks—Giant-sized children's blocks, usually made of board, make marvellous visual-aid devices.

You just paste a sign on the front of each block (and a number on back so that the speaker gets the sequence right.) Instead of putting signs on a board, he stacks the blocks up point by point.

It's a very colorful device and more interesting-looking than a board. You could always use the closing sign-line: "And that's how we build a structure of solid sales" or some other building-oriented phrase.

SALES MEETINGS

You can use flash cards, like those schoolteachers use to teach the multiplication tables, or slides, or movies. You can rent slide projectors and make your own slides with special pencils. There are any number of visual aids you can make out of readily accessible materials. Just look around you, and be creative and unafraid. It doesn't have to be elaborate.

THE SECRET OF A SUCCESSFUL CATALOG   13

*The buying/
selling tool*

"Sales are a disaster. We'd better tell those salesmen to get off the golf links and start pushing in the field."

Nervous management always looks for a fall guy for falling sales, and inevitably the initial scapegoat is the salesman. It does seem logical to blame the order-taker for not taking orders. However, jumping to conclusions in business can be a dangerous and costly exercise. Being too quick to settle on the cause for slower sales prevents the thorough analysis of other factors which may be the real cause of the trouble.

One of the prime failures of small-company management is not backing up its sales forces with the proper tools, and the prime sales tool is the company catalog.

The catalog is the very heart of a company's total selling effort. It is, in effect, the salesman's bible; he lives or dies by it in the field.

Ideally, the catalog should function in a two-pronged way to secure business: (1) as a selling tool for the salesmen and (2) as a buying guide for the customers. This may sound like fancy semantics, but it's not. It involves a specific approach to the presentation of the company's products. A poorly arranged, confusing catalog that is incorrectly oriented can virtually cripple salesmen and prevent them from working at peak efficiency.

HOW TO PLAN AND ORGANIZE THE CATALOG

Group Products According to How They Are Used, Not How They Are Made

Products that are made together should not necessarily be sold together. How, where, and by whom the merchandise or service is used are the only factors that determine catalog groupings.

You may have two products that are virtually identical, except one has a widget on top for home use and the other has the widget on bottom for industrial use. Now, most nonpromotion-minded executives tend to say: "Why waste catalog space and repeat the specifications twice? It's really the same item—just show one picture, and mention that it comes in two variations."

Fine. They've saved space and lost sales for both products. The buyer who is looking for a home widget gets thrown by an industrial-looking item and the buyer seeking an industrial widget says, "That's not for me—that's a home product." So by cutting catalog space costs, they also have cut the catalog's selling effectiveness.

You must think in terms of how the buyer thinks and buys, and address yourself solely to his needs. Because two products are made with a similar manufacturing technique, or because they happen to be fashioned of the same material, or have any other production similarities is of absolutely no interest to the buyer. When he's looking for a specific item, he expects to find it under the specific use category.

For instance, suppose you are preparing a retail jeweller's catalog and wish to advertise some gold charms that could be used on a woman's bracelet or on a man's neck chain. The expeditious space-saving way would be to show the charms and state, "For Men and Women." Sure, why not? It's the same item, isn't it?

But the real question is: Would a male buyer be likely to find it in the ladies' charm-bracelet section of the catalog? If he's looking for a medallion to suspend from his chain, he wants just that, and not an "also." The right place to feature it is in the men's jewelry section, among the cuff links and signet rings. In other words, show the same piece twice, or three times, categorized according to its uses and users.

A clever merchandiser like Bergdorf Goodman of Fifth Avenue in New York, demonstrated this specialized user approach by running ads that featured "Men's Gold Medallions" in a series before Christmas.

These were actually the same medallions that were being sold as charms in the women's jewelry department. Result: doubled sales for the same item by capitalizing on its doubled use.

If you were preparing a catalog for a toys and hobby-goods wholesaler, and you have a butterfly net that is also used as a fish-tank scooping net, would you show it in the fish-tank equipment section or in the butterfly-catching equipment section? The answer, of course, is show it in both sections with a completely different sales pitch each time, because the fellow looking for a fish-tank net is going to hit the fish-tank section only, and the butterfly-catcher is not going to go flipping through the entire catalog to figure out where you might have put his net.

Buyers are the busiest of people—and the least patient. They are not going to take the time to figure out puzzles or listen to salesmen's lengthy explanations. If they don't see what they are looking for fast, they'll pick up someone else's catalog. So categorize products according to appeal, not appearance. Place each item where the buyer expects to find it—not where it is convenient or economical for you.

Group Products According to How They Are Bought

This calls for putting yourself in someone else's head. You have to figure out how a buyer thinks when he is planning a purchase of your particular type of product. Does the customer buy in terms of style, price, size—or what? Every field is different, and the best way to find out the buying idiosyncrasies of your industry is to tackle those walking treasure troves of market information—the company salesmen.

Talk to the salesmen, chat with the order clerks—anyone involved with taking orders. Find out just how customers *ask* for your products, and arrange your catalog groupings accordingly. For instance, suppose you're offering some sort of monthly service, such as office maintenance, or bookkeeping, or public relations. You may learn that the question most commonly asked by potential clients is: "What can I get for about $200 per month?" Perhaps you are cataloging eyeglass frames. The salesmen might mention that most customers want to know which frames they can get for under $100. Maybe you are with a food importer whose customers frequently ask for gourmet foods that retail for under five dollars. If price turns out to be the major purchasing factor in your field, then the wisest thing would be to group your products or services according to cost. For instance, a page devoted to $50 spectacles, another page showing $90 eyeglasses, and so on.

In the ring-binder field, buyers think in terms of soft cover or hard cover, three-rings or multi-ring. So if you were preparing a ring-binder catalog, you would group products according to these elements. Now, that may sound like simple logic. When you realize that this means a single binder cover becomes four different products and should appear in four different places in the catalog, you may have some idea of the problems ahead.

For as I've mentioned, working in small- or medium-sized businesses means you are usually working closely with production managers and other nonpromotion-minded management. All they know is that this is the same binder cover, with some minor variations.

You have the task of explaining that each variation transforms it into an entirely different product: a soft cover three-ring, a hard cover three-ring, a soft cover multi-ring, a hard cover multi-ring. You can see where you may have some difficulty in conveying your concept, but don't let them deter you. They may know how to make it, but you know how to market it.

In the lamp trade, people generally buy according to incandescent and fluorescent. There are many other selective factors, of course, but that's the basic one. And that would be your primary cataloging division. In a furniture catalog you would probably classify according to style periods—contemporary, provincial, and so on. In publishing you would undoubtedly arrange according to subjects.

How to Use Suggestive Selling

Remember the days when if you asked the druggist for a toothbrush, he suggested toothpaste? And when you bought shoes, the dealer asked if you needed polish or shoe trees? And if you bought shelving paper, the dealer asked if you needed thumbtacks?

That's called suggestive selling, and it's still one of the most effective ways of upping a sale. You can apply this technique when you are preparing a catalog by showing interrelated products together. If there are accessories involved with a product, show them on the same page.

If it's a toy catalog, list batteries next to all battery-operated toys. If it's a calendar catalog, list refills right along with the bases.

This is the simple procedure of reminding the buyer of related items that he might need in conjunction with the purchase he has just made. He's happier that you performed the service of advising him of what he will need to have the item he's just bought work properly. And you're happier because you have achieved the greatest possible buying potential from the catalog.

Of course, this does not preclude the necessity of featuring these same accessories in their own combined category Thinking in buyer's terms again, remember there are many times that a purchaser merely needs refills or accessories (sometimes even for someone else's products, but why be proud—a sale's a sale). He should not have to figure out where you have placed them. A page or section headed "Accessories" will take him right to it.

Mix and Match Products

Okay, you've found the right way to group your particular items, and it works. What's to stop you from also having a few pages of alternate groupings to pull more sales mileage out of the catalog?

Say you have arranged products according to style. It might be a good idea to introduce a page of "under $50" items. This especially is effective in retail catalogs, much as department stores set up "Gifts under $50" and "Gifts under $10" tables around Christmastime. It facilitates selection by the many ambivalent customers who know what they want to spend but not what they want to buy.

If you have used price as your grouping basis, have a page or two of selected items that conform to one style or type: For lamps it could be "Student Lighting Suggestions"; for furniture you might have "Young Homemaker Styles." Perhaps you might just single out particular good buys from each section of the catalog and create a special category called "Especially Good Values."

Diversified Catalogs Can Create New Markets

Most companies love to put out one big catalog consisting of everything they make. They're proud of their whole line and want to impress customers with the sheer volume of their output.

As a result, a prospective purchaser of, let's say, industrial building adhesives may have to wade through pages showing jeweller's cement, library glue, and other items of total disinterest to him. Chances are he won't even bother, but if he does, he's not impressed; he's distressed. The company has wasted the costs of cataloging and mailing unnecessary pages and has possibly destroyed the sale by catalog overkill.

There is absolutely no purpose in lumping everything together under one cover merely because they are made under one roof. Each market should have its own catalog, with products described in terminology familiar to that market. Here's how the diversified-catalog technique can be used to create new markets.

We had a client who had commercial ring binders that were also sold as photo albums. They knew there was a large market for albums, yet their sales in the photo field were negligible. They asked us what we could suggest in the way of promotion to increase their album sales.

Since the catalog is usually the key to a company's approach to marketing, that's the first place we looked. There was the answer. Each page showed a stark ring binder and carried the legend "Used for home and office, for sales presentations and photos."

Simple, neat, and from the manufacturer's point of view, what could be better? But from the buyer's point of view, nothing could be worse. For one thing, since the catalog was originally and principally aimed at the office-equipment field, specifications were oriented to the commercial buyer. Capacity was shown in terms of how much data and how many charts the binder could hold. Terms were used such as "ring mechanism" and "gauge acetate." Adjectives such as "tough, heavy duty."

Now, when people want a lovely, sentimental photo album, they don't want a durable ring binder. It's all in the adjectives—what attracts one buyer repels another. True, the company salesman would tell his retailer customers that these binders were really exactly the same as albums, but how would that help the retailer when *his* customer asked questions? The catalog must provide the retailer with the familiar terminology that enables him to present the selling points within his customers' frame of reference. If you handicap him with the necessity of translating, forget it—you've lost the sale.

All we did was to make a separate catalog for photo albums. The same commercial binders were shown, but did they look different! They were pictured in decorator settings, described from the use and viewpoint of a photo album (i.e., capacity in terms of how many snapshots it stored).

Suddenly the firm had a full line of photo albums. Their salesmen were now equipped with a specialized selling tool that enabled them to approach photo shops and talk in their language. Result: A new market was opened that became a very lucrative source of sales.

Sometimes you can get an idea for a new market potential in the wildest way. I was visiting a friend in the hospital once and happened to notice that the lamps over her bed and on the mobile examination table were made by one of our clients. When I later mentioned this fact to the client, he said: "Sure. We make special voltage and wiring adaptations of many of our regular lamps for hospitals."

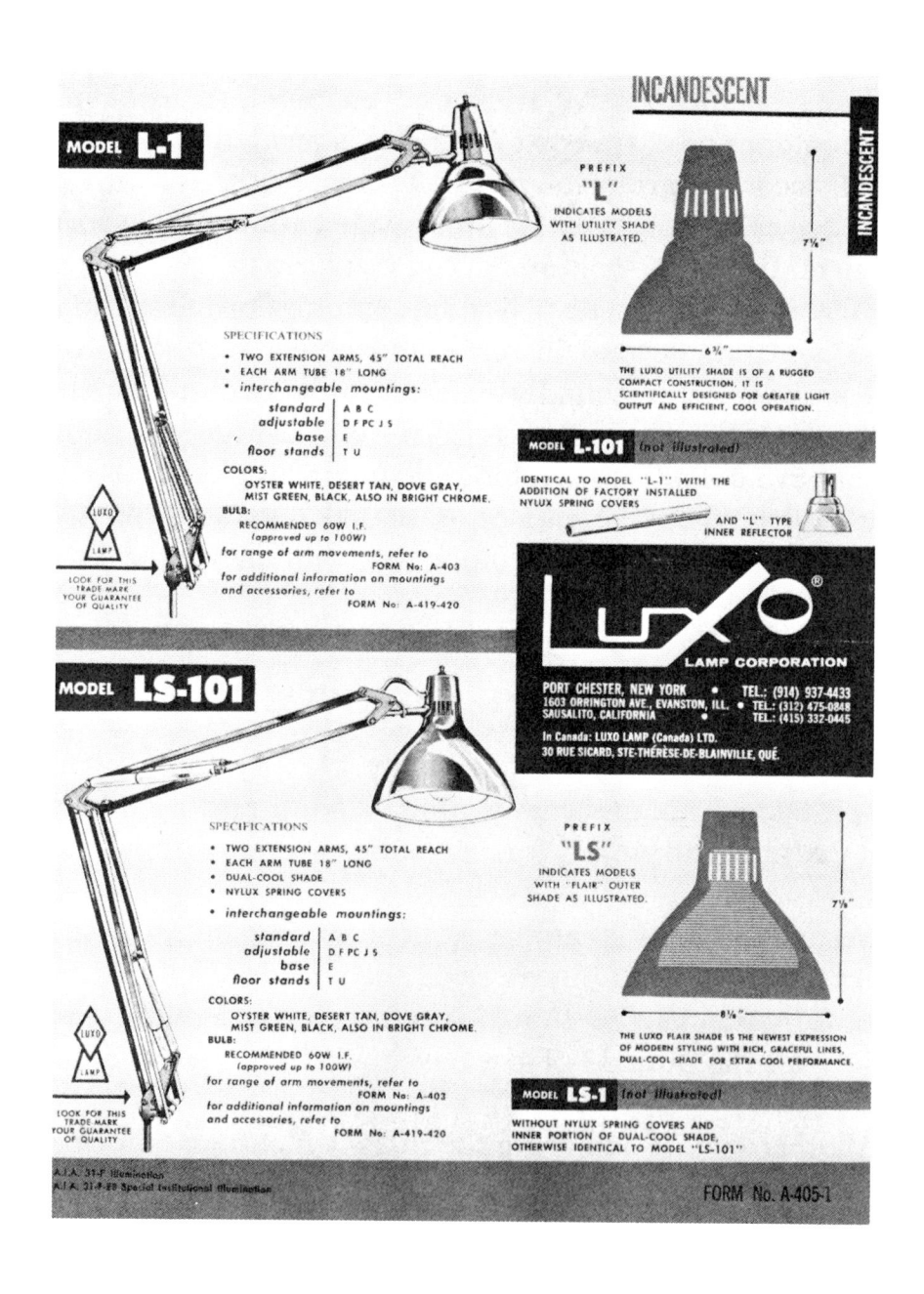

Before: Note the lack of cohesion. The specifications and features are scattered about so that the eye doesn't know where to settle. Also observe that pertinent information about accessories is shoved into various corners. And, finally, the line art of the lamp shows nothing of the true look of the product.

L-1, L-101* series
The Classic Shade

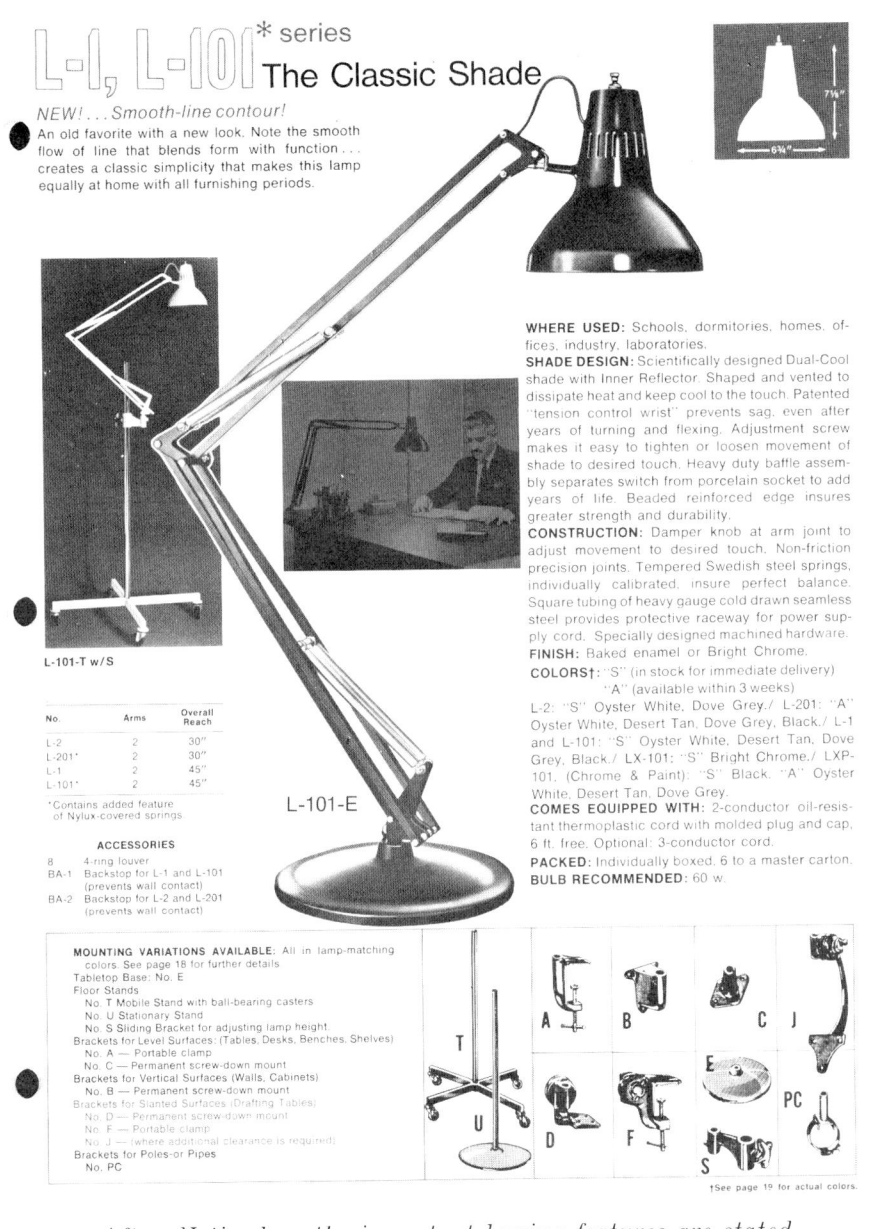

NEW!...Smooth-line contour!
An old favorite with a new look. Note the smooth flow of line that blends form with function... creates a classic simplicity that makes this lamp equally at home with all furnishing periods.

L-101-T w/S

L-101-E

No.	Arms	Overall Reach
L-2	2	30"
L-201*	2	30"
L-1	2	45"
L-101*	2	45"

*Contains added feature of Nylux-covered springs.

ACCESSORIES
8   4-ring louver
BA-1   Backstop for L-1 and L-101 (prevents wall contact)
BA-2   Backstop for L-2 and L-201 (prevents wall contact)

WHERE USED: Schools, dormitories, homes, offices, industry, laboratories.
SHADE DESIGN: Scientifically designed Dual-Cool shade with Inner Reflector. Shaped and vented to dissipate heat and keep cool to the touch. Patented "tension control wrist" prevents sag, even after years of turning and flexing. Adjustment screw makes it easy to tighten or loosen movement of shade to desired touch. Heavy duty baffle assembly separates switch from porcelain socket to add years of life. Beaded reinforced edge insures greater strength and durability.
CONSTRUCTION: Damper knob at arm joint to adjust movement to desired touch. Non-friction precision joints. Tempered Swedish steel springs, individually calibrated, insure perfect balance. Square tubing of heavy gauge cold drawn seamless steel provides protective raceway for power supply cord. Specially designed machined hardware.
FINISH: Baked enamel or Bright Chrome.
COLORS†: "S" (in stock for immediate delivery)
"A" (available within 3 weeks)
L-2: "S" Oyster White, Dove Grey./ L-201: "A" Oyster White, Desert Tan, Dove Grey, Black./ L-1 and L-101: "S" Oyster White, Desert Tan, Dove Grey, Black./ LX-101: "S" Bright Chrome./ LXP-101. (Chrome & Paint): "S" Black. "A" Oyster White, Desert Tan, Dove Grey.
COMES EQUIPPED WITH: 2-conductor oil-resistant thermoplastic cord with molded plug and cap, 6 ft. free. Optional: 3-conductor cord.
PACKED: Individually boxed, 6 to a master carton.
BULB RECOMMENDED: 60 w.

MOUNTING VARIATIONS AVAILABLE: All in lamp-matching colors. See page 18 for further details.
Tabletop Base: No. E
Floor Stands
  No. T Mobile Stand with ball-bearing casters
  No. U Stationary Stand
  No. S Sliding Bracket for adjusting lamp height.
Brackets for Level Surfaces: (Tables, Desks, Benches, Shelves)
  No. A — Portable clamp
  No. C — Permanent screw-down mount
Brackets for Vertical Surfaces (Walls, Cabinets)
  No. B — Permanent screw-down mount
Brackets for Slanted Surfaces (Drafting Tables)
  No. D — Permanent screw-down mount
  No. F — Portable clamp
  No. J — (where additional clearance is required).
Brackets for Poles or Pipes
  No. PC

†See page 19 for actual colors.

After: Notice how the important buying features are stated instantly. There is a convenient table at the bottom, and all accessories are grouped together under the heading "MOUNTING VARIATIONS AVAILABLE." Also notice how the dimensions of the lamp are used as a design element in the upper corner of each spread.

151

STEP-BY-STEP ADVERTISING

Following up on that casual lead, we culled all the lamps, plugs, stands, and accessories that were applicable to the hospital and medical field and created a special "Hospital and Medical Lighting Catalog." This led to the establishment of an entirely new sales division and a new and extremely profitable market for the company.

A cookware manufacturer might put out a separate catalog for industrial cookware equipment. A food broker might put out a catalog of organic foods. A bank might put out a catalog of "savings and money-management plan for widows."

The possibilities are as unlimited as the applications of the products or services you are selling.

HOW TO ARRANGE THE CATALOG

All too often, the writer of a catalog is so enamored of the sturdy construction features of his product or the fine way it performs its functions that he forgets to stess what the function *is*.

The prime rule in writing a catalog is the old cliché, "First things first." There's no point in telling someone how great your product is unless you tell him what it's for!

When a buyer is flipping through a catalog, he is seeking specific information, and he wants the facts fast, without digging through tons of flowery verbiage. If dig he must, forget it. One of the most frequently committed catalog sins is the burial of vital product specifications in a solid paragraph of prose. A catalog is no place to go creative. There is a basic framework that must be followed—a consistency of style that the buyer can rely on. He wants certain facts about every product and wants to see them in the same place on each page. This gives an orderliness to the catalog that facilitates ordering procedures.

The introduction to the catalog is the institutional image-building "see how great we are" pitch that should appear on the inside front cover. It is usually the part of the catalog read more carefully, and more agonized over by the head of the company. Remember, this puts into words all the pride he feels over his accomplishments and status.

Here is a good place to have a picture of the plant and/or offices; shots of employees at work; a map pinpointing international distribution. Whatever elements you can conjure up that will represent the position of the company in the industry.

If you really want to pour it on, you can have a heartwarming "message from the president." You'd be surprised at how many people read it, besides the president and his mother.

The basic facts about ordering, terms and buying conditions, should be shown immediately, usually on page two or three, often next to the table of contents. F.O.B. where, company policy about returns, shipments, and so on.

How to Analyze Products for Buying Features

Before setting up the individual pages, it is necessary to analyze the underlining features of each product. Again we turn to the poor man's market research bureau—the company salesmen. Go over your current catalog with them, and find out what specifications customers want most to know about each product.

The basic questions most prospective purchasers want answered are:
1. What does the product do?
2. Where is it used, and by whom?
3. How does it do it better than the competitive products?
4. How is it made?

These are the selling points that will convince him of the value of your products. Now he's ready for the specific selection process. Now he needs the buying features—construction factors he must know to get the version that most closely meets the need of his situation. This means colors, capacities, how it's packed, what it comes with, etc. If you want a simple guide as to what "buying feature" information should be included, just think of what facts your shipping or billing department needs for processing an order.

The Page Setup—What appears on top of each page to instantly identify each product should appear consistently in the same form, in the same spot, on every page. One of the most frequently used headings is the model number of the product followed by its name. It might read, "Model 756 The Windsor Series."

Now, why not just state the name, and leave the model number for the tables? Because usually no one knows the product name except the boss and his wife. In a small business, the job of making up names for products is usually placed in the creative hands of the head bookkeeper or someone equally qualified. That's why you get such a redundancy of product names in many industries. How many times have you seen heavy-duty products named Hercules; or a classy product named Majestic; or a service company called Acme?

The purpose of the page heading is instant identification, and the most commonly used name *among the buyers* (not the sellers) should be used.

Following the heading is the descriptive data. Here you might start with some prose, just a few lines generally extolling the lead features of the product. Then come the details. Using the information gleaned from your analysis of buying features, evolve a basic format of captions that can be applied to every product, arranged in order of their importance. An example for a lamp catalog would be: where used; shade design; construction; finish; colors; comes equipped with; packed; bulb recommended.

The ultimate distillation of information is the ordering table and is usually the second thing looked for on each page. This table should be at the bottom of each page, with columns arranged in order of ordering details: (1) model or style number, (2) size, and (3) description.

It's easier for the buyer to have price right along with the product specifications, and in a retail catalog that's mandatory. These days, with the tremendous fluctuation of prices in raw materials, many companies find they cannot afford to get locked into a list price for the life of a catalog. So if you are in an industry that has to accept price fluctuations as a fact of life, prepare a separate price list that can be changed often with economic feasibility.

One of the handiest devices, and most frequently used in the entire catalog is the back-page index. It involves a tremendous job of collation but is well worth it. It is simply a listing of all the company's products in *numerical* or *alphabetical* order. Four columns that state: model number, price (if included), shipping weight (if an important buying consideration), and last, the page number on which the item appears in the catalog.

Now, this may seem like a nothing, but I have seen this index page face up on more desks than any other part of the catalog. Think of the convenience and ready reference it offers. Most customers, company employees, and sales clerks know the company products by style or model number. This index gives them an instant method for finding a specific product.

HOW TO DESIGN THE CATALOG

The cover is the grabber. After all, that's what stops them; that's what encourages and invites a buyer to open your catalog. That's why the design is vital.

If the design can integrate a representation of your products, fine. But that should not be the governing factor—not if it harms the design potential of the cover. Just be sure it is strong and hits hard like a billboard.

Now the inside. Here you must think in terms of *spreads*, not single pages. Remember, the eye sees both pages simultaneously and should therefore be considered as one design entity.

Simplicity and *good photography* are the imperative factors. Too many design gimmicks can overpower the data you are presenting. Keep it clean, clear, and simple, and clear, factual photography is vital. This again is no place to get too arty—not if it obscures the product in any way. The prospective customer wants to see what he is buying in as sharp detail as possible.

Black-and-white catalogs can be quite smart. If that's what the budget dictates, contrasts can be achieved by reverses (white on black) or bendays (greys).

Color can be a most effective device in a catalog layout and design. Not only does it break up the monotony, but it can be used to give a change of pace subjectively as well as aesthetically. For instance, you can single out important selling points in color, or you can consistently put all refill information in color. You can distract from the sameness of two items by silhouetting one against a color and showing the other against white.

Here's an inexpensive trick that enables you to have a third color at no extra cost. A catalog is printed in "forms," which means a group of pages. There are three forms of eight pages each in a 24-page catalog. Each form is run on the press separately. You can have the printer run each form in a different two-color combination: first one in black and red, second in black and green, third in black and yellow. He is actually printing only two colors at a time, so that's all you pay for. (He will charge you about $35 for washing up the press after each run.) When the catalog is bound together, you will have a multi-color look that is attractive and impressive.

HOW TO MAIL THE CATALOG

The envelope should immediately identify the contents as a catalog. This prevents the recipients from putting it aside and possibly burying it forever under a pile of third-class mail.

No one discards a catalog. It is of immediate interest to everyone it goes to. Buyers need them and look for them, because catalogs are the tools of their trade. Just state boldly on the outside of the envelope: "This is your *New Catalog 833.*"

Another way of achieving the instant identification effect is to use

DEALER CATALOG SHEET
1964-65 SEASON

PRATT'S FRUIT TREE SPRAY

The new formula contains Captan 6.0%, Methoxychlor 10.0%, Malathion 6.0% and Sulfur 25.0%. One pound mixes with water to make 12 gallons of spray. (5 tbs. per gallon of water) The inclusion of Sulfur in this formula gives miticide properties and powdery mildew control which the other materials alone will not do.

SIZE	RETAIL PRICE	DEALER PRICE	CASE PKG.	SHIP. WGT.	PROD. NO.
1 lb.	$ 1.39	10.01 doz.	12	15 lb.	1516
3 lb.	3.69	13.28 case	6	25 lb.	1548

PRATT'S TOMATO & VEGETABLE DUST or SPRAY

The 3/4% rotenone and 7% copper dust used by vegetable gardeners for many years is now also packed in this handy dust gun. This all-purpose Bug-Blight dust controls insects and fungous diseases on grapes and small fruits, as well as on tomatoes and other vegetables. Used as dust or diluted with water for spraying. 1 pound makes 10 gallons of spray.

SIZE	RETAIL PRICE	DEALER PRICE	CASE PKG.	SHIP. WGT.	PROD. NO.
½ lb. gun	1.00	7.20 doz.	12	10 lb.	1808
1 lb.	1.00	7.20 doz.	12	15 lb.	1816
3 lb.	2.39	8.60 case	6	25 lb.	1848

Both 1 lb. and 3 lb. packed in canisters

PRATT'S 72% CHLORDANE

The complete "Do it yourself" termite-proofing directions appeal to every house owner. Additional label directions are given for control of household insects, such as ants, roaches and spiders. Grub-proofing of lawns and spraying of ornamentals are also covered in the directions. Also effective as a crabgrass preventative.

SIZE	RETAIL PRICE	DEALER PRICE	CASE PKG.	SHIP. WGT.	PROD. NO.
8 oz.	1.98	14.26 doz.	12	14 lb.	2408
1 pt.	2.98	10.73 case	6	13 lb.	2416
1 qt.	4.98	17.93 case	6	25 lb.	2432

Larger sizes on bulk list

PRATT'S 6% CHLORDANE DUST

Kill lawn, soil, garden and household pests with Chlordane. Apply 1 pound of Chlordane per 600 sq. ft. for lawn and soil insects. Dust foliage with shaker canister or gun for garden insects. Control roaches, ants, silverfish and carpet beetles indoors by dusting Chlordane in places inhabited by bugs.

SIZE	RETAIL PRICE	DEALER PRICE	CASE PKG.	SHIP. WGT.	PROD. NO.
1 lb.	.79	5.69 doz.	12	15 lb.	2616
4 lb.	1.75	12.60 doz.	12	52 lb.	2664

Prices of larger quantities on request.

B. G. PRATT COMPANY, 204 TWENTY-FIRST AVE., PATERSON, N. J. 07509

Before: Products of unrelated categories are thrown together, which makes no sense to the customer seeking a specific group of product. Product descriptions are vague and do not contain all the facts. Notice how much space is wasted on the price tables—almost one-half the page. Line drawings of products look unreliable since they represent only the artist's conception.

INSECTICIDES SPRAYS
for trees • shrubs • evergreens • flowers • vegetables • ornamentals

B G PRATT SINCE 1904

Fruit Tree Spray
Special Pratt 3-in-one combination . . . insecticide, miticide and fungicide. Controls insects & diseases!

DESCRIPTION: Captan, Methoxychlor, Malathion and Sulfur in a wettable powder form. GENERAL DILUTION: One pound makes 10 gallons of spray.

FOR CONTROL OF: Insects — aphids, cankerworms, tent caterpillars, red spider mites, leafhoppers. Diseases— scab, powdery mildew, brown rot, botrytis rot.

WHERE USED: Apples, pears, peaches, plums, cherries, strawberries.

WHEN USED: Throughout season. Prior to blooms opening, at petal fall and about 10 to 20 day intervals throughout the season observing time of last spray before harvest.

PACKED: Canisters and bags.

No.	Size	Case Pkg.	Case Wt.
1516	1 lb.	12	15 lbs.
1564	4 lb.	12	50 lbs.
1525	25 lbs.	1	26 lbs.

Rose & Flower Dust or Spray
2-way protectant . . . controls insects and diseases!

DESCRIPTION: A proven formula containing Sevin®, Malathion, Kelthane® and Folpet. A complete insecticide, miticide and fungicide. Mixes with water for spray, or ready to use as dust. GENERAL DILUTION: One pound makes 10 gals. of spray.

FOR CONTROL OF: Insects — aphids, leaf rollers, Japanese beetles, lacebugs, mites. Diseases — black spot, powdery mildew, leaf spot.

WHERE USED: Roses, flowers, and ornamentals.

WHEN USED: Throughout the plant-growing season.

PACKED: 10 oz. size in handy refillable squeeze-duster. Also 1 lb. canister and 4 lb. bag.

No.	Size	Case Pkg.	Case Wt.
1610	10 oz.	12	10 lbs.
1616	1 lb.	12	15 lbs.
1664	4 lbs.	12	50 lbs.

Tomato-Vegetable Liquid Insect Spray
A spray concentrate for broad spectrum vegetable insect control.

DESCRIPTION: Contains 20% Methoxychlor and 10% Diazinon® GENERAL DILUTION: One fl. oz. in 5 quarts of water covers vegetable garden area of 545 sq. ft. (25' x 22').

FOR CONTROL OF: Aphids, cabbage worms, flea beetles, leafhoppers, corn earworms, grasshoppers, Japanese beetles, cucumber beetles, squash vine borers, serpentine leaf miners, fall army worms.

WHERE USED: Tomatoes, broccoli, cabbage, corn, cucumbers, melons, peas, squash, radishes.

WHEN USED: Throughout growing season when insects appear. Observe intervals between last application and harvest.

PACKED: In bottles. Larger sizes available as Methoxy-Diazinon 20-10 EC on Bulk List.

No.	Size	Case Pkg.	Case Wt.
7108	8 oz.	12	12 lbs.
7117	1 pt.	12	20 lbs.
7132	1 qt.	6	20 lbs.

Diazinon® 18E Insect Spray
The multi-purpose spray for turf, foliar and nuisance insects.

DESCRIPTION: Contains 1.5 pounds Diazinon® per gallon. GENERAL DILUTION: 1 tablespoon per gallon of water.

FOR CONTROL OF: Chinchbugs, beetle grubs, aphids, mites, leafhoppers, spiders, ticks and earwigs.

WHERE USED: Lawns, fruits and vegetables, flowers, shrubs. Also sprayed on window frames, doors, screens, foundations, walks, garbage cans.

WHEN USED: Whenever signs of infestation appear.

PACKED: In bottles. (Larger sizes available, see Bulk Price List.)

No.	Size	Case Pkg.	Case Wt.
18608	8 oz.	12	11 lbs.
18617	1 pt.	12	20 lbs.
18632	1 qt.	6	19 lbs.

Please read product label for specific directions.

After: Products are grouped according to buying categories. Descriptive copy for all products is uniform; vital data are called out consistently so the customer can instantly find the item needed to solve a specific problem. The price tables are neat and readable without overpowering the page. Actual photos of the products are used, not unrealistic line drawings. (Reprinted by permission from Henry Pratt)

STEP-BY-STEP ADVERTISING

Pliofilm polyethylene bags for mailing. A number of magazines are now mailed this way, with address labels affixed in the corner. The advantage is apparent (pun intended). The recipient sees what it is the minute the catalog hits his or her desk.

Many companies like to enclose a letter. If there is something to be said that cannot be included in the catalog, such as price structure, new corporate policy, etc., this is the place to state it. However, it had better be important to warrant the additional expense of inserting, plus printing.

Of course, you want to call attention to new products; buyers like to know of that at once. In fact, "What's new?" is usually the first question they ask when presented with a new catalog. You can call out the new products on a memo that may be clipped to the catalog or inserted in it. But again, this is a costly affair. Also, the "new" signal can be indicated with graphics on the catalog pages themselves.

Don't forget the order cards! Since you've spent a whole catalog presenting and selling your wares, it would be gross folly to overlook giving a method of buying them.

It's true that many buyers prefer to send in orders on their own purchase-order forms, but there's nothing handier and more conducive to buying than bound-in order cards.

The form is pretty simple—just columns for style number, quantity, etc. Here is the place to add that important line: "Please send me —— additional copies of this catalog."

There are undoubtedly many other members of the customer company who have buying influence (for instance, their own salesmen). The more catalogs you have in effective buying hands, the more merchandise you will sell.

Avoiding Postal Perils

Here's a bit of advice that can save you heartaches, headaches, money, and maybe your job.

Before you go ahead with any printing or purchasing, have a dummy facsimile made of the entire catalog mailing. The printer will make up a bound dummy on the exact weight paper proposed. The envelope maker will give you a sample of the exact weight envelope you plan to use. Then insert a dummy memo, letter, order cards—whatever you intend to include in the catalog mailing—and take it to your local post office for their okay.

You may be shocked to find that two pages less or a slightly lighter weight paper will make a huge difference in postage cost. The inclusion of a letter may change the postal classification and throw you into a more costly category. Of course, they'll tell you the current regulations for specifications that must be printed on the envelope to ensure the return of undeliverable catalogs. They are too costly to be lost forever in dead mail.

Postal authorities can be quite sticky, arbitrary, and implacable. I've heard stories that would make strong men blanch. Like the company manager who learned, after the catalogs were all neatly sealed and stamped and delivered to the post office, that his last-minute addition of four pages moved the catalog into the next mailing class, which cost five cents more per envelope. When you're mailing thousands of catalogs, that runs into big cash.

HOW TO CUT DOWN CATALOG ERRORS AND COSTS

There is some perverse chord in human beings that causes them to relish the discovery of errors in printed material, especially catalogs. Mistakes are bound to occur in a compilation of data as extensive as a catalog. No matter how carefully one checks and rechecks, some point will be overlooked.

To reduce mistakes, here's the fail-safe procedure I have always followed. When you have completed the first copy draft of the entire catalog, photocopy it, and distribute copies to every conceivable individual in the company who can come down on your head later (and incidentally, whose opinions and advice may be very helpful). Write the person's name on his copy—that puts him on notice that opinions are being recorded for posterity, and if he overlooked something now, he can't holler about it later. Then attach a note asking for opinions, suggestions, etc., and demand a "must be returned by" date.

When you have your first set of proofs in hand, follow the same procedure. You may have to pay the printer for a few extra sets of proofs, but it's worth it. At this point those interoffice nitpickers can be invaluable as proofreaders because they are looking only for errors, while you have been evaluating content.

After you have all copies returned and have integrated all valid corrections, then and only then, go ahead and print. The day that the new catalog is distributed in the office, make up a brand-new big file folder ostentatiously labelled "Next Year's Catalog." Then when the first character comes in to gloatingly point out the error he found on page 21, you can thank him coolly, and with great aplomb slip his notation into the folder and continue with your work.

WRITING A SALES LETTER 14

How to get readership and response

It's Monday morning, and you're in the midst of trying to find your desk under the pile of morning mail and to adjust your weekend metabolism to the weekday tempo and a salesman walks in.

"Good morning, valued customer," says he with a smile, "I want to thank you for your favors, past, present, and future."

What would you do? Probably after checking the outer office to see if his keeper is waiting, you'd chuck the nut out.

Now, if that's how you would handle a man talking like that, think how fast you would dump a letter that rambled along in that archaic jargon.

Yet, for some unfathomable reason, businessmen persist in loading their letters with stilted, antiquated language that conjures up images of clerks in celluloid cuffs.

There seems to be some misconception in the halls of commerce that phrases like "We humbly beg your indulgence" or "We are deeply grateful for your past business" give the business letter a dignified, impressive tone. Maybe it did 50 years ago, but today that kind of talk is anachronistic and totally ludicrous; especially when these expressions of craven humility come from some crude commercial cutthroats who couldn't care less if you dropped dead—as long as it wasn't in the middle of the season.

The language in any letter should be succinct, simple, and to the point. You have something to say—that's why you wrote the letter in the first place. Then say it straight out, and don't entangle your statements in a mass of rhetorical sludge.

THE SUREFIRE FOUR-STEP SYSTEM FOR SUCCESSFUL SALES AND LETTERS

Like most things, it's easy to write a successful sales letter once you know what to do and what not to do. I've just told you what not to do; now let's get to the "how to's."

During my years of writing sales letters and teaching others how to write them, I have evolved a system of rules—an outline to follow when composing and creating sales correspondence. I guarantee that if you follow this procedure, you will turn out the best, most effective sales letters you have ever produced.

Step 1. The pull-in. (Grab attention instantly.)

Step 2. Make your point. (Announce your offering and extol its benefits.)

Step 3. Tell him what he must do to get it. (Where, how, how much.)

Step 4. Impel him to do it right now.

Now let's take it step by step.

Step 1: The Pull-in

Every letter must begin with an attention-grabber—the means of beguiling the reader to read on. We can divide these devices into two categories: gadgets that cost and gimmicks that don't. Naturally, since this book is designed for the economy-minded entrepreneur, we'll begin with the second category—gimmicks that are free and easy.

It's amazing how many simple things you can do to a letter to make it distinctive. Remember that distinctive merely means different; anything that can be readily differentiated from its peers is automatically distinctive. Among the guests at a Park Avenue dinner party the man of distinction would be the one in an undershirt. If sloppiness causes instant standout, we can use it to advantage in sales letters.

Fingerprints and Smudges—Most mail arrives in pristine condition, carefully typed and neatly spaced. Think of your double take if you opened an envelope and drew out a letter that was decorated with a few large smudges and finger marks. (Notice I said "a few." Don't get carried away and turn the page into an unappetizing, unreadable mess.) There are a number of transitional lead-ins you could then use. For example, if you were promoting a hairdresser or a clothing store: "Your fingerprints are unique, distinctively, personally you. Just as your hair style (or clothes) should be individually, personally you."

If you are advertising a repair or maintenance service of any kind: "Does it pay to dirty your hands on repairs that you really are not equipped to handle? Why not let a professional do the job?"

If you were promoting protective plastic envelopes: "Grime doesn't pay. If that thumbprint obscured a critical digit in a job specification, you could have a $1,000 error. Protect your job tickets in plastic envelopes."

Cutoff Corner—Here is a very simple trick that makes any letter instantly different. Just have the printer slice a diagonal piece from the top corner of the sheet. Think of the many ways you can use this device to lead into a telling point. Try this for openers: "There are many ways for manufacturers to cut corners, but this is the *only* way you will ever see *us* do it."

Think of the many ways you can use this opening to unleash a blast at price-cutting, corner-cutting competition that you've been dying to tell off for years.

Or: "Trying to cut corners to make ends meet? Why not let us help out with a loan to tide you over until...."

Handwritten Letter—Who says a sales letter must be typewritten? Among the usual run of neatly typed letters, the casual quality of a handwritten message is a sure stopper. Print it in blue ink on yellow blue-lined legal-pad paper, and you convey an intimacy that will be extremely effective.

Of course, the tone of such a letter must be informal. None of that "Gentlemen: In response to yours of the 5th." Keep it casual—the sort of thing that might conceivably be construed as a first-draft hastily-jotted down interoffice memo. That doesn't mean it must be you who does the jotting. If your handwriting, like mine, resembles the berserk meanderings of an ink-covered centipede, shop around for local talent. Check the office for some nice mature person who went to school in the days when the Palmer Method meant penmanship and not golf.

Underscores, Call-outs, Arrows—Circle an important point, underscore it, or just draw a freehand arrow. Make some marginal handwritten

WRITING A SALES LETTER

notation like "Don't forget this!" Have the printer reproduce these callouts in blue or red, so that they look like they've been actually inked in. These break up the monotonous look of a letter, giving it a rough and readable quality.

Irregular Spacing—A mass of aligned words looks tidy but dull. Avoid an appearance of total sameness. There are no points awarded for neatness or consistency, so juggle things around a bit. Indent a few lines that make a particularly telling point. Make one paragraph narrower and line it up all flush left. Make another one narrow, all flush right. The important thing is to keep the eye moving, to make the page varied and aesthetically interesting.

Skip the Salutation—"Dear Sir" or "Gentlemen" or "Dear Customer" hardly add a personal touch to the letter. So why bother? A letter can be a letter without a salutation. If it appears on letterhead paper, with a signature beneath, that conveys a letter. Try starting your letter with a catchy headline.

The Personal Story—Comedians make their living mocking themselves; why not letter writers? Begin with some personal difficulty that you beseech the reader to help you solve. For instance, it's always open season on henpecked husbands, shrewish wives, nagging in-laws, and so on. It gets you instant interest and amused sympathy.

I once used this device successfully in a letter that was sent out just before the company catalog. The purpose of the letter was to pave the way for the soon-to-be-mailed catalog, to prime the customer for its imminent arrival. The success of the letter, and the fact that it was read, was proved by the tremendous number of personally directed comments that began to show up on orders.

Rye, N.Y. 10580

Please—save my home life by reading the new V.P.D. catalog that you will receive soon.

My wife, Cynthia Smith, has been slaving away over this new catalog for the past six months. She's worked like a dog, and I've lived like one. Nothing but frozen foods for dinner and cold silence for company while she devoted herself completely to describing the glories of the tremendous range of new and old products.

Now after all the effort—can you imagine what it will be like to live with her if the catalog is not a success?

So please, for pity's sake—*read it carefully.*

It will be for your sake too, because you'll find the new catalog will be a most valuable buying and selling tool. It will be a pleasure to use because:
1. It's step-indexed, enabling you to turn to the product category you seek in seconds.
2. It's the only catalog of its kind to contain everything you need in plastic products and presentation binders.

As you can see, I've caught some of Cynthia's tremendous enthusiasm for V.P.D. products. But that's nothing to what I'll catch from her if her catalog is anything less than a tremendous success.

So I beg you—when you get the new Joshua Meier V.P.D. catalog within the next few weeks, please *read it carefully and buy.* Cynthia will be watching the mail anxiously. The smooth flow of my home life will be determined by the flow of your orders. *Please—read and then write . . . right away!*

With heartfelt thanks,
Sincerely yours,
David Smith (Cynthia's husband)

The results of this letter were overwhelming. We received mail from customers beginning "Dear Dave, Don't worry." For years after, people I met in the industry would ask with sympathetic concern: "How's Dave?" The fact of the matter is they became personally involved, and that's what you want to effect. If I had sent a straight letter that said, "We are sending out our new catalog soon so hold off and don't buy from our competitor yet," do you think anyone would have read it?

Step 2: Make Your Point

I have a standard technique for instant improvement of almost every sales letter. Just cut off the opening paragraph, and bring the closing one up to the top. Try it. Nine out of ten times, you'll have a better, more forceful letter. Many people have a squeamishness about coming right to the point.

In Eastern countries it is considered the height of business boorishness to plunge into crass commercial discussion immediately. One must pursue a ritual of deference and delicacy, and the topics of trade may never be touched upon until after the second cup of tea. It's a lovely and gentle way of working that never quite took hold here. Somehow, I can't quite visualize a salesman delicately balancing a porcelain cup as he discusses the history of civilization and the state of his wife's health with a smiling, courtly purchasing agent. A paper cup of lukewarm instant coffee while they haggle over price, maybe.

Hereabouts, you get down to basics fast, on a call or in a letter. If you put off the point, you put off the reader. Patience is not part of our commercial culture, and delay means death. You must convey the main idea of your letter immediately, or the busy reader may never wait around to find out what it's all about.

After the hopefully provocative lead paragraph, describe your offering. Simply, factually. What it is, how the reader will benefit.

Step 3: Tell Him What He Must Do to Get It

How much does it cost? What does he have to do to get it? This is the nuts-and-bolts information the reader needs to buy. If there's an order card enclosed, tell him.

Step 4: Impel Him to Do It Right Now

This is the crucial point—the activator. If your letter has been successful, the prospect wants to order by the time he reaches the end of the letter. Now we're in the danger zone. Will he buy now, or will he put the letter aside to attend to later? If he puts it down, you're through. Later means maybe, and maybe usually means never. The letter gets buried beneath the next day's mail and the next day's, and soon it becomes part of a messy pile that gets thrown out in bulk.

You must create the push to act immediately. "Order now, because this is a *limited offer,* good only until . . . ." This is the standard technique, and it works surprisingly well. Give a cutoff date or some imposed limitation that will mean they risk missing out on this great opportunity unless they *act now.*

Another strong simple way is just to say it straight: "Delay, and you may miss out on this tremendous, once-a-year opportunity. Don't put this letter down until you have sent in your order!"

All you must remember when you close a letter is, if you want the order, it's *now* or never!

Here is an actual sales letter given to me for some "improvement" by a

STEP-BY-STEP ADVERTISING

sales manager. It is a perfect illustration of the kind of garbled material ground out every day by small company executives who are totally uninstructed in sales-letter writing.

It's a classic case of what not to do and why everyone who is responsible for creating commercial correspondence should get some training (or at least read this book!).

To a Valued Customer!

We are enclosing our new Kleer-Vu price list which covers our entire packaged line of report covers, page protectors, pencil cases, photo accessories, and our award-winning wallet inserts.

Your profit on this Kleer-Vu line represents one of the highest levels in the industry, and we want to play a game with you in the hope that you'll expand the number of our items you are carrying.

The game which we call our "Lucky Seven-Eleven Promotion" will bring you only prizes and profit. It costs nothing to play, and it's very easy to be a winner.

Write an order for seven out of the 59 items that are on the price list for a total of $700, and we will send directly to you or anyone you designate an AM/FM clock radio in a radical new, cube design. This item has a retail value of $59.95.

If you can use more than seven items, write an order for 11 items totalling $1,100, and we will send you, or anyone you designate, a beautiful AM/FM stereo with eight-track tape receiver built in. This will come complete with matching two-way horn speakers.

Kleer-Vu wants you to have these items both as a thank you for past business and as an incentive to add more of our very profitable items to your line.

The rules of the game are simple: (1) Call your Kleer-Vu representative right now or write the order and send it directly to this office. (2) Be sure your order covers seven items and totals $700 if you want the digital clock radio. (3) Make sure that your order totals 11 items and is for a total of $1,100 if you want the AM/FM stereo. (4) Be sure your order calls for delivery prior to April 15.

WRITING A SALES LETTER

Fill out clearly on your order, or on the attached form, the gift you want and the name and address of the person you want it sent to.

Both of these prizes are great for your office or your home—the Kleer-Vu line is great for your profit and has been known for years and years for the best customer acceptance in the industry.

We've got a quality product and we count on you—our distributor—to sell it. This is our way of thanking you for favors past, present, and future, and we certainly hope you'll play our "Lucky Seven-Eleven" game with us.

Our best regards, and we hope you have a banner year.
Sincerely yours,

Now let's tear it apart.
1. Note the hot salutation and sparkling opening paragraph.
2. Note how much monotonous verbiage has to be penetrated before you reach the point of the letter—that this is a promotion that offers valuable free gifts.
3. Note the phony ring of the sixth paragraph: "We want you to have these items as a thank you for past business." Nobody buys that sanctimonious stuff. It introduces a hypocritical touch that threatens the credibility of the entire letter.
4. Note the waste of good "hook:" "Be sure your order calls for delivery prior to April 15." A weak throwaway of the order-impelling fact that this is a limited offer.
5. Note the trite do-nothing closing, which maybe doesn't matter, since I strongly doubt that many people would ever read down far enough to see it.
6. Note how many words were used to cover what could be said in half the space.
7. Note the use of the celluloid-cuffs school of language: "To a valued customer!" "Thank you for past business." "This is our way of thanking you for favors past, present, and future." "Our best regards, and we hope you have a banner year."

Are you getting any guilt pangs as you read this letter? How many times have you loaded your correspondence with this sort of useless verbiage?

Okay, that was the "before." Here's the "after"—and the actual letter that went out:

Abe says I'm nuts.

"Give away radios, stereos? And to customers who are already buying Kleer-Vu products? Why?

Because I want to induce you to buy even more! That's why I created this *Lucky Seven-Eleven Promotion*. It's simple, it's great, it costs you nothing. And look what you get absolutely *free:*

You buy seven items, for a total of $700, and *you get* an AM/FM Digital Clock Radio in a smart new cube design . . . retail value $59.95—*free.*

You buy 11 items, for a total of $1,100, and *you get* a stunning AM/FM stereo with eight-track stereo cartridge player and matching two-way horn speakers . . . retail value $129.95—*free.*

That's all there is to it.

Just look over the enclosed *New Kleer-Vu price list* which covers our entire packaged line of Report Covers, Page Protectors, Pencil Cases, Photo Accessories, and our award-winning Wallet Inserts.

Then pick out seven items totalling $700, eleven items totalling $1,100 . . . and we'll send your beautiful, valuable prize to you or anyone you designate. But do it now, because this is a *Limited Time Offer!* Orders must be for delivery before April 15.

Use the handy enclosed order form. Mail it to us, or phone your order to your Kleer-Vu representative.

But do it right away, please. I'm anxious to show Abe who's really nuts around here.

Sincerely yours,

Now that you've read it, can you believe it covers exactly the same points as the "before" letter? Let's see how it follows my four steps of sales-letter writing:

Step 1: The pull-in. "Abe says I'm nuts." Note the personal touch that draws the reader into the immediate involvement. Why should Abe say, "I'm nuts?"

Step 2: Make your point. By the second line the reader knows he can get free radios and stereos. The purpose of the letter and what it offers are immediately apparent.

Step 3: Tell him what he must do to get it. You buy, you get, and see what it's worth. This is the heart of the letter—the pulling power; thus it is sharply delineated, indented, and set up to stand out.

Step 4: Impel him to do it right now. The limited-time offer, plus the personal plea, ends the letter with a hook couched in a smile.

And notice the immediately stated purpose of the promotion at the beginning of the letter: "Because I want to induce you to buy more." This sets a note of deliberately disarming honesty which adds acceptability to the entire letter.

And the spacing: Note the judicious use of indentation and varied-size paragraphs to make the letter look more alive and inviting.

Now look at the length of the letter. Everything has been accomplished in under half the space of the "before" letter.

Here you have seen an example of how to apply the four-step system to a sales-letter problem. It is merely a matter of organizing what you want to say into sales-inducing sequence, distilling the message, eschewing the clichés, jettisoning the flowery do-nothing prose, and setting the letter up in a smart and interesting fashion.

Whenever you are preparing a sales letter, follow the four-step guide, and you really can't miss.

COLORS, PAPER, AND PERSONALIZING

There have been all sorts of direct-mail surveys and studies made on the value of color in sales letters. Red, blue, and black ink on white paper seem to have the edge.

But that's when you're talking about mailing a half-million straight-sell letters in a cold call mail-order effort, where every fraction of a cent counts.

My own experience has shown that in small-scale efforts the ink color is just one element in the pulling power of a sales letter. Basically, the letter rises and falls on what it says and how it says it. Of course, it must make an initially appealing, attractive, and readable impression.

A good stock, rag bond or laid finish, is important to give substance and importance. There's nothing that invites instant oblivion faster than an all black-ink letter on shiny cheap sulfite bond. Not only will the letter be ignored, but the company that sent it will be written off as some fly-by-night organization that is hanging in by nickels and dimes.

The idea of any sales letter is to cleave as closely as possible to the individually typed look. In this computer-crazed era that converts people into numbers everyone welcomes any indication of personalization. Even though you know, deep down, that the letter you receive is but one of thousands, the little delusion that maybe it was prepared especially for you always exists.

That's why a letter should look typewritten, with a signature, and any underscoring or marginal notations printed in blue ink. It's bad enough to know that you're not important enough to warrant a personal letter, but at least you have sufficient standing for the sender to go through the effort of trying to make you think you are. A blatantly mass-printed letter relegates the recipient to a position of total insignificance. It clearly shows the disdain of the sender. And if the sender doesn't care enough to send the very best, why should the reader bother to buy?

The pinnacle of personalization can be achieved by word processors. These machines individually type letters and stop to insert specific names and addresses—all automatically. If you have your own such machine in the office, you can easily turn out these wonderfully presentable and effective letters. If not, check around the local letter shops; you're bound to come across one that performs this service.

There are no hard and fast rules for determining the length of a sales letter. Letters that come with appeals for subscriptions to periodicals invariably cover two to four pages. The magazines and book clubs have learned that an in-depth description of what they're offering is necessary to convince an individual to spend the money for subscriptions. Remember, these letters are going to homes, where the living is easier, and there's time to sit and study the letter during television commercials.

If you are selling a product or service that goes to the home—a security system, air conditioning, a pool, a sprinkler system—a long letter is a must.

Tell your story, reiterate the benefits, repeat the construction features, hit away at the economies, stress the conveniences—take all the room you want to convince the prospects that they urgently need your product or service.

Home readers need more persuasion than office readers. The purchasing agent who decides within minutes to issue orders for thousands of dollars of merchandise, equipment, and supplies will agonize for weeks at home over the decision to invest $150 in a lawn mower. Of course, that's *his* money he's spending, which accounts for the intensified caution. As in a fancy restaurant, you can always spot the fellow on an expense account by the cavalier glance he accords the check; but when it's on him, watch the scrutiny and careful tabulating that goes on.

WRITING A SALES LETTER

A letter going to places of business is different; brevity, clarity—just the facts, ma'am. Nobody working at today's frantic business pace has the time to mull over mail. Tell it fast, and tell it strongly—get in and out—because the meter is ticking.

POINT-OF-PURCHASE DISPLAYS 15

The selling moment of truth

When you walk into a store, I bet you think it's just a store. Well, it isn't. It's actually a business battlefield you're treading on, with every square inch of floor and counter space fought for ferociously by thousands of manufacturers, wholesalers, and distributors.

This is the final proving ground. It is the point of purchase, where the final truth must be faced: Will the consumer buy your product or service?

The first hurdle has been overcome: You have sold your goods to the wholesale buyer or to the retailer, but only because you have convinced them that your product is appealing, valuable and saleable. Now you had better prove it by getting the stuff to *move*.

The point of purchase, the selling floor, is your last push-off point. Everything you have done up to now—advertising, promotion, public relations—all can be lost unless you catch the elusive eye of the ultimate buyer and impel him to reach for your product and make the purchase.

Once upon a time you could depend upon store salesmen to explain and sell. Today, most stores are self-service, whether or not they intend to be. The days of salesmen who care are over. If you care to move goods, you must join the battle for the floors, walls, counters—and may the best display win.

HOW TO KNOW WHEN YOU NEED A DISPLAY

When one of your salesmen bursts into your office frantically hollering: "Acme just put out a gorgeous floor display and they loaded all my customers with merchandise, and I can't write an order to save my life!" then it's too late.

Unfortunately, in small business everyone is too busy just coping with the everyday aggravations of getting the work done, the merchandise shipped, and the bills paid to give thought or time to such exotica as point-of-purchase displays. It's the kind of subject that gets put off "until we get the chance to talk it over." However, when the competition hits the field with a display, suddenly it's panic time. Then the display salesman, who had been trying to make an appointment with the sales manager for five months, is summoned into emergency session.

What kind of display do they want? Just like the competitor's, of course. Only better, more beautiful, and cheaper.

A "me too" display will get you nowhere. It makes the company look second best and sell second best. If ever you are forced into that position of counteracting a competitive unit, at least make yours different. There are many approaches to every display situation. Avoid the temptation to imitate.

But why allow yourself to get put into that bind? The time to think about a display is now.

SITUATIONS THAT SCREAM FOR DISPLAYS

Selling a product to a buyer is hard. Selling a selling unit is easier. When you come into a new market and want to introduce your line, offer it in a display unit. The buyer will be more willing to take a chance on an item that you have packaged to sell itself.

No store salesman is going to stand around and explain the virtues of your new product, no matter how great and unique. If you don't inform consumers of its existence and tell them the marvellous things it can achieve for them, your new creation will remain unsung, undiscovered, and unsold. You must accompany every new product with some sort of point-of-purchase education device—some means of telling the selling story.

If you have the kind of product that is stocked away on shelves, awaiting requests from the purchaser who is lucky enough to find a salesperson who will reach for it, getting the stuff onto the selling floor can change your entire sales picture. A display can make your merchandise visible and accessible to the browser and buyer.

Every dealer has his favorites—the items in your line that he has been buying for years. It's hard to get him interested in the many other good or different numbers you make. He's loath to get involved in new stock numbers, new inventory. Why rock the selling boat? Here's where a display can do the job. Create a unit that carries an in-depth selection of your products, and you make it easy for him to expand his purchases—and sales—of your merchandise.

It's Mother's Day, graduation, or spring cleanup time—or just a two-for-one offer. A special promotion must have a special display to remind the store personnel as well as the customers.

HOW TO DECIDE WHAT KIND OF A DISPLAY TO USE

First off, you must case the field you plan to hit. In what kind of market will the display appear? Mass merchandisers, supermarkets, novelty stores, pharmacies, specialty stores, Mom-and-Pop stores, wholesalers' showrooms, filling stations, beauty shops—wherever.

Each market has its own particular set of specifications, and if you don't conform, you're dead. For no matter how stunning—even if it walks, sings, and talks—if it's the wrong dimensions or the wrong type of unit, it will never reach the selling floor.

There are four ways to find out the special display demands of an industry and to evolve the best kind of unit in which your merchandise should be presented to that field.

1. Trade associations. Every industry has its trade association. Contact them and tell them your problem. They can provide invaluable information about the design limitations and specifications of the industry, if there are any. Some of the larger ones will supply you with printed material that establishes display guidelines.

2. Your salesman. Talk to your men in the field, or if you're planning to enter a new field, talk with the sales representatives you intend to engage. Find out what sort of displays are around, which they have noticed are more effective, and what the competition is doing.

3. Trade magazines. Take a space salesman to lunch. He is a walking encyclopedia of promotional advice.

4. Hit the road yourself. This is the big "must." Get out and get around, to small stores, in urban areas and suburban areas and small towns. Look around, inspect, chat with dealers and store personnel. Just don't open by asking a direct question like "What kind of display do you think we ought to make?" You'll get the blank look that masks the mental confusion most people experience when confronted with a question that requires a creative opinion. On the other hand, you may be subjected to a dogmatic discourse by some self-appointed retailing expert who never allows his ignorance to deter him from giving assertive advice.

Just ease your way around, examine the store displays, and ask opinions of the value of the various types you see. Find out which kind sells, which kind the store manager likes and why. Notice the position awarded each display unit, and analyze why one kind gets better billing than another.

After you have completed your research, you will have formulated some ideas as to the kind of display unit that would work best in your market—for your type of product—for your specific promotional need.

TYPES OF DISPLAYS AVAILABLE

The cigar-store Indian, the barber pole, the pawnbroker's ball trio—these are all point-of-purchase displays. Anything that creates interest and moves goods at the point of sale is, by definition, a point-of-purchase display.

There are five main types of displays: signs (indoor, outdoor, clocks, decals), counter displays, floor units, wall-hung displays, and ceiling-hung displays. They can be made of any of the following materials, listed according to cost, starting with the least expensive.

1. Cardboard
2. Corrugated board
3. Wire
4. Masonite
5. Sheet metal
6. Wood
7. Plastic

Each type of material lends itself to different situations. Now let's go into the many ways and whys of using the various fabricating elements available.

STEP-BY-STEP ADVERTISING

Cardboard and Corrugated Board—the Cheapies

A mounted reprint of an advertisement is the simplest and cheapest display possible. If you have run a consumer ad, you can have the magazine run off extra copies and mount them for you. This is effective at the point of purchase because it reminds buyers who may have seen the ad that "Oh, yes—that's the gizmo I wanted to see."

Or if you have printed a selling sheet that's attractive, simple (not cluttered up with paragraphs of small type and dealer terminology), and *consumer-oriented,* you could have it mounted and easelled into a display. Frankly, I hesitate to even suggest this, because I have seen too many purely industrial catalog sheets that have been mounted, sent out, and thrown out. It's a terrible temptation, I agree, to try to amortize the expense of the printing and preparation of a dealer catalog sheet by deluding yourself into thinking it can perform double duty.

"It shows the product, it tells the price—what more does a display need?" Plenty. It needs a reason for the consumers to buy. It needs applications that are recognizable to them. It needs big pictures, big type, and a design that should be visible from across the store.

You can prepare a catalog sheet with that double use in mind and save money, but you must plan for it beforehand. For instance, we made a catalog sheet to introduce a new lamp for the student market. One side was totally consumer-oriented, with a series of photos showing the lamp being used in student-type situations. The other side had dealer information—packing, discount, colors, etc. The dealer got the two-sided sheet. The consumer side suggested to him why the lamp would be bought and how his store personnel could pitch it. For consumer display use, we printed a few thousand one-side-only and had them mounted.

Perhaps you have a one-cent sale offer or a two-for-one deal or a special-time-of-the-year bargain. Then it pays to have a counter card made up for the occasion, but only if it is for limited-time-only use. Displays are highly expendable, and number one on the discard list is the counter card.

This sort of display also could be made of vacuum-formed plastic, which is feasible in quantities of two to three thousand. It could be used to display the product, such as having a niche in which the product fits. So the sign becomes an effective demonstrator display for counter or window.

If you're lucky enough to have a tiny product that can be mounted en masse on a card (razor blades, batteries, flints, etc.), you can use a counter card as a dispenser display.

The small display cards that are clipped on the ends of supermarket shelves are known as shelf-talkers. They're good for limited specials, since they will be kept around for short terms only.

You see self-shippers everywhere, everyday. These are shipping cartons that convert into counter (or sometimes floor) displays. A few dozen assorted to the box. Dealer opens box, folds cover in half, thereby exposing printed display material, tucks it into the back of the box, and—*poof!*—it's a display, filled with merchandise and ready to sell.

It's about the simplest, least expensive way to create a self-service display. This is ideal for small merchandise assortments on a counter. For large, heavier products, the same concept can be used with a corrugated floor unit. This is called a dump display and is quite popular with mass merchandisers. Just be sure to check size specifications here. The supermarkets, who are big users of dump displays, will not accept anything over waist height (24 to 36 inches square is the popular size), and the sign that stands up in back can be no taller than 60 inches.

Of course, you realize that self-shippers are self-disposables. When the merchandise is finished, so is the display. On the plus side you avoid the follow-up problem of keeping the display stocked; on the other hand, it's a one-shot deal, which means the cost of the display must be paid out of the profit on the contained merchandise. You can't amortize the unit from future business that comes from refilling, as with permanent displays.

Wire—Efficiency without Elegance

Sometimes display-suppliers get fancy and call these wrought iron, but they're just plain bent wire. A wire display is about the cheapest permanent unit you can get, although it doesn't have to look it. A smartly designed sign and brightly colored wire (it has to be dipped to make it black anyway, so why not use blue, yellow, or red instead?) can make the unit reasonably attractive.

They fold nice and flat, are easy to ship, and are a snap to set up (which is an important factor). They can be made counter-size, floor-style, or wall-style to fit on a pegboard.

Wire displays are inoffensive and functional, but they have no class. So if you are selling high-ticket merchandise, wire is not the way to go.

Wood, Masonite, Metal, and Plastic—the Quality Look

Now we're getting into the top-drawer department—the displays that convey high-level quality, value, and style, and of course, carry a high-level price tag.

A wooden display can cost anywhere from $15 to $100. I've seen manufacturers pale visibly at the suggestion of giving away such expensive units to their dealers. "Why the hell should I pay for furnishing the dealer's store? It's his fixture—why shouldn't he pay for it?"

There are a few answers to that oft-heard plaintive plea. First, he doesn't *have* to pay for it. There are hundreds of suppliers just pleading to give him displays. Second, you are not furnishing his store. In fact, you are not giving him anything—*he* is giving *you*. You are, in effect, leasing space in his store to sell your product. It's strictly a real-estate transaction, and he's in the seller's seat. Third, there are painless ways of splitting the cost with the dealer that can work out quite nicely. We'll get to that shortly.

The basic display used in all self-service stores today is called the gondola. I don't know what romantic soul applied a name that conjures up soft images of sailing along under moonlight to a bulky unit that stands and sells under fluorescents. The gondola fixture ranges in height from 54 to 60 inches, is sheathed in pegboard, comes with standards and shelves, and is finished off at the bottom with a kick base.

A variation of this unit is your best bet, since it is most readily adaptable to all retail outlets. Remember, that's the important consideration.

A floor-display unit is an investment. It should be used to create a complete self-service selling center for your merchandise, where a consumer can see, pick, and choose the exact version he needs. It is the best way to get your products onto the selling floor in a more conspicuous, heavily trafficked location.

Moreover, it's forever. It's permanent and can produce sales for years to come.

THE NO-RISK WAY OF BUYING DISPLAYS

The one thing you don't want to do is order 200 displays and then find out that nobody wants them. There are prescribed ways of hedging your bet and avoiding the risk of the unknown, of ascertaining the acceptability of the display beforehand, of knowing in advance how many display units you will be able to sell.

When you have decided conclusively that you need and want a display, here is the procedure to follow:

Select a point-of-purchase supplier. There are hundreds and hundreds of companies who design and produce displays. Select a few, and call them in to discuss your specific problem. When you have arrived at the one you feel is most experienced, helpful, and creative, ask them to submit a few sketches.

Show sketches to selected big buyers. There's nothing more flattering than to be placed in the role of respected expert, and that's the position in which you place a buyer when you ask his opinion on the value of your projected display. Their advice and suggestions can be an invaluable contribution. After all, they deal with displays constantly and are fully familiar with what's good, bad, and needed. You're in good shape from a future selling point of view, too, because their involvement in the creation of the display almost ensures their ultimate purchase of it.

Have a prototype made. The display company will set a price on the manufacture of a single prototype which covers their costs fairly. The usual practice is to credit that charge towards your order. In other words, if you do not go ahead with the production, you pay for the sample unit. If you do go into production, the sample is free.

Have photographs of the prototype made. Show the actual prototype at trade shows, furnish photographs of it to salesmen, send out mailings on it, and write up orders with a promise of delivery within a few months. You will then be in the lovely safe position of knowing exactly how many displays to buy and in no danger of being stuck with a warehouse of unwanted displays.

"How much can we afford to spend on a display?" is a frequently asked question, and there's a variety of answers. The rule of thumb is 10 percent of the total net cost of the initial deal that goes along with the unit. In other words, you give away $10 for every $100 worth of goods purchased.

However, what you really should ask is how can you afford not to spend on a display? A permanent display unit is an investment. It is an annuity that will continue to produce income. As to who carries the expenditure, it is customarily chalked up to the advertising department or the sales department of your company, depending upon who loses the fight.

THE NO-COST WAY OF BUYING DISPLAYS

There is a juggling money technique that works quite well with display deals and ends up with neither you nor the dealer paying for the unit. That's what it seems like, but it's like a shell game. Actually, it's the dealer who pays, but in such a psychologically effective way that it doesn't hurt a bit.

Here's how it works. Say the display has cost you $15. This is how you present it to the dealers.

New Introductory Display Deal

You buy ...	$150 net worth of merchandise
You pay ...	$20 for the display
You get free	$20 *retail* worth of merchandise to cover your cost of the display.

After you have sold the $20 worth of goods, you have made the cost of the unit; thus the display costs you nothing.

To the dealer, it looks like fancy bookkeeping, where on the one hand you charge for the display, and on the other hand you give him the means for making the money to pay for it.

For you, the display is totally free. The economics are like this: The free merchandise (that retails for $20) costs you around $5, right? The display costs you $15. The dealer has paid you $20. Thus the display cost you $0!

It's a lovely arrangement and one that is used by many companies very successfully. Of course, there's a fallacy. The $20 retail worth of merchandise normally costs the dealer $10, or whatever his discount brings it down to. So you are really giving him $10, not $20, which means he is paying for the display. But it doesn't feel like it, because he doesn't have to put out a dime—and psychologically, that feels like free.

PROMOTE YOUR P.O.P.

It's new, it's great—it's the hottest thing to hit the selling floors since pipe racks. That's the story you want to get across—and *quick*.

Send out mailings, feature the deal in trade ads, but blanket the field fast. This has to be engineered and planned as if you're General Patton, with surprise and speed as your prime strategy. Once your competition gets wind of the display that threatens to displace and overshadow their line, you can bet that they're not going to sit still and watch you move in.

So before they can marshal their forces and come up kicking, clawing, and fighting with deals, offers, and other retaliatory razzle-dazzle, you had better be sure you have saturated the field and have achieved complete coverage.

While the display is still in the design stage, you can prepare your promotion plans. You might consider "spiffs" for your sales force—a bonus for each display sold—or sales contests among them, maybe with a premium gift for each six sold and a top prize for the one who sells the most.

Develop a six-month program; keep it lively, and keep it moving. Your aim is to maintain a high pitch of interest and enthusiasm among your salespeople and customers. After all, no matter how great a display is, it won't produce a nickel unless you get it out into the performing arena. So talk it up.

HOW TO BE SURE YOUR DISPLAY KEEPS ON SELLING

Lights, Action

To shed light on your merchandise is lovely. Built-in lighting can be a plus factor for your display if you are selling to dealers in downtown areas. They can then use the display as a night-light, and you have the advantage of your name in lights 24 hours a day, visible to all.

However, the era of downtown business is ebbing, and the pleasures of evening strolling have been destroyed by fear. An electrified display requires proximity to an outlet, which poses a problem of positioning in the store. Then, you run into the penny-pinching retailer who complains about the costly electricity being consumed. So all in all, electricity is a needless expense.

Action and motion are great attention-getters, albeit a bit costly. Jumping figures, rotating products, and other movements can be achieved with electricity, but then you have the problems mentioned before. Battery-operated motors are available at fairly low cost, but you must accept the reality that when the battery dies, so does the display. No dealer will bother to replace a battery.

No Dogs Allowed

One slow mover can kill an entire display. I know it's tempting to try to pass off a few "dogs" when arranging an assortment—a tie-in package forcing the dealer to take the bad with the good. However, it can destroy the effectiveness of the unit, and the only one penalized is you. A good display contains a balanced assortment with quantities of each item determined by its popularity. Twelve of the fast movers to one of the slow numbers, or whatever is a realistic appraisal of their sales-moving potential. In theory, the perfect display assortment empties from the shelves in unison.

Don't Let Ego Reign

The suggestion may arise in the executive office to throw a sample of everything the company makes into a display. It may do big things for the boss's ego to show the world what a grand, big line he produces, but it will do very small things for sales. Arrange your assortment fairly. Put in only what you know the dealer can move in his particular marketing arena. The determining factor is sales, not ego.

The Rule Is Realism

If you're working with a modest volume field, like small specialty stores, what's the point of setting up a display deal that requires an initial order of $700? You'll only scare off the little guys and cancel your cause. Sure, it would be nice to make up the entire cost of the display the first time around, but reality must rule, or the display will never get to work for you. Evaluate the dollar amount that is acceptable to the market you are aiming for, and set up your merchandise deal accordingly. Be patient; you will make up the cost in time as the display produces sales for years and years.

Pilfer-Proof Means Sales-Proof

The buyer wants your display to be pilfer-proof and asks you to package the product so that it is inaccessible. He also would like you to figure out a way to protect the product from ravages of customer handling. In the next breath the buyer tells you that the merchandise had better sell. So where are you? If you close off the products so that they're unattainable and seal them in so that they're untouchable, how will people buy them?

One idea is to have samples on display and boxed stock below. But don't bank on this method as the solution. Customers have been known to open boxes to examine the product and then insist on a fresh clean unhandled one. So the answer is, don't worry. Your prime aim is to sell. Put the stuff where everyone can get to it, and let the store managers worry about pilferage and handling.

No Riders Allowed

It hurts to see competitive merchandise on your display. Yet it's a natural procedure for the dealer to put similar items together and a common tactic of competitors to try to hitch a free ride on your unit.

Some of this is inevitable, and you may take some comfort in the fact that your name appears on the unit and the predominant proportion of contents will always be yours. Sometimes you can cut down on this competitive incursion by designing the display in such a way as to accommodate your goods only.

For instance, if you have packaged your products in a unique shape, it's easy to have hooks that support only that shape. Perhaps your boxes vary in dimensions; build the shelves to accommodate your sizes only.

As I said, some infringement is inevitable. By considering this problem beforehand and making a pointed effort to tailor your display and make it unsuitable for anyone else's merchandise, you can cut down on free riders somewhat.

Keep It Clean; Keep It Filled

What's more dreary-looking than a half-empty, dusty display? Or more aggravating than seeing empty, useless shelf space that could be featuring and selling your goods? Servicing displays is a problem, and you must keep on top of it with periodic prodding.

Keep nudging your salesmen to visit every store to which they've sold a display. Urge them to see that it's tidy and filled. Point out that the only way to get the full profit benefit of this nice steady business-builder is to keep replenishing the merchandise that's moved. Give them a proprietary feeling about each unit they place; make them realize that they have a vested interest in maintaining these "assistant salesmen."

Keep a record of every store that has a display, and send periodic reminders and order forms to the store managers. Maybe give some sort of incentive—a special personal gift—to the manager, or an extra discount refill deal.

The main point to remember is that placing the displays on the dealers' floors is not the end of your or the salesmen's responsibility—it's only the beginning.

Index

AA's, 57
Advertising
  effectiveness of, 109–110, 111
  services, 61–66
  terms, 57–59
Advertising space salespeople
  as source of market data, 28
  as source of trade publication data, 43
Age markets, 18
Alcoa, 55
Alka-Seltzer, 21, 22
Attitudinal research, 31–36
Avery Fisher Hall, 69

Bacon's Publicity Checker, 101–102, 105, 107–108
Bargaining, 63, 66
Benday, 57
Bergdorf Goodman catalog, 145–146
Better Homes & Gardens, 48, 49, 50
Binding, 59
Bleed, 59
Blueprint, 59
Brand names, 40
Bridal market, 51–53
Brynner, Yul, 104
Budget, 37–38

Camera-ready, 59
Catalogs, 144–159
  arranging, 150–154, 156–157
  checking for errors in, 159
  designing, 154–155
  diversified, 148–149
  importance of, 144
  mailing, 155, 158–159
  planning, 145–149
  product information to include in, 153
  suggestive selling in, 147–148
Celanese Corporation, 54
Chambers of commerce, 24
Circulation of magazines, 43, 48
Cliches, in advertising copy, 76–77
Coated stock, 59
Color
  in direct mail pieces, 86–89
  in sales letters, 169
Comp, 59
Company salesmen, 18, 24–26
  See also Salespeople
Consumer magazine advertising, 48–53
Cooperative advertising, 53–55
Copywriting, 69–77
  cliches to avoid in, 76–77
  emotional appeal in copy, 75–76
  honesty in copy, 70, 76
  humor in copy, 73–74
  innovations in, 77
  and size of ad, 70
  steps to writing ads that sell, 70–73
  tips on, 73–77
Corporate image craze, 67–68
Creativity, in advertising, 59–61

Die-cutting, 59
Direct mail advertising, 78–93, 111
  with business reply cards, 93
  color printing in, 86–89
  envelope ideas, 85–86

185

INDEX

letter folding techniques, 82–85
and newsletters, 90–93
paper for, 89
with postcards, 86
quiz included in piece, 89–90
repetition in, with different colors, 90
using familiar objects in unfamiliar places, 79–82
vs. trade-paper advertising, 40, 41
Direct response advertising, 44
Displays, point-of-purchase, 172–183
Distribution of products, 18–19
DuPont, 55, 136

Economic markets, 17
Emotional appeal, in advertising, 75–76
Expenditures, 37–38

Focus groups, 31–36
discussing price of product in, 34–35
moderator, 35
participants, 35–36
procedure for, 32
questions to ask in, 33–34
taping, 32–33
Font, 59
Frequency, in advertising, 45
Frigidaire, 40

Galley proofs, 57
Geographic markets, 18
Glossary of production terms, 57–59

Halftone, 57
silhouette, 59
square, 59
Honesty, in advertising, 70

House Beautiful, 48, 49
Humor, in advertising, 73–74

Image, corporate, 67–68
Industry statistics sources. *See* Market data sources
Institutional advertising, 39–40

Jewelers' Circular Keystone, 23
J. Walter Thompson, 54

Kleenex, 40

Laid finish, 58
Layout, 58
Life magazine, 50
Lincoln Center, 69
Line copy, 58
Lithography, 58
Logo, 58
Lowenbrau, 55

Magazine advertising, 111
consumer, 48–53
frequency of, 45
position in, 45–47
repetition of, 47
and size of ad, 45
trade, 39–48
Magazine Networks, Inc. (MNI), 49–51
Magazines
circulation of, 43, 48
regional, 47–48
Manufacturers' representatives, 18–19
Market data sources, 22–30
company salespeople, 24–26
order clerks, 29–30
retail salespeople, 26–28
space salespeople, 28
suppliers' salespeople, 28
trade publications, 22–24

INDEX

Market research, 16–36
  analyzing sales, 19–22
  and attitudinal research, 31–36
  determining markets, 17–18
  and numbers research, 30–31
  product distribution methods, 18–19
  reference guide, 24
  sources of market data, 22–30
Markets, 17–18
  age, 18
  bridal, 51–53
  economic, 17
  geographic, 18
  professions, 17–18
  trade, 18
Matte finish, 58
Mechanical, 58
Media mix, 111
Media selection, 111
  consumer magazines, 48–53
  direct mail, 78–93
  institutional advertising, 39–40
  newspapers, 111
  radio, 109–112
  television, 111
  trade publications, 39–48
Merchandising advertisements, 53
Metropolitan Home, 49
Mezzotint, 58
MNI (Magazine Networks, Inc.), 49–51
Multilith, 58

New product introductions, 41
Newsletters, 90–93
Newspapers, 109–110, 111
News releases, 94–108
  circulating release, 107–108
  ·discovering new markets for, 101–102
  with photograph, 98
  preparing, 95–98
  and press parties, 105–107
  what to publicize, 98–101
  writing when nothing is happening, 102–105
Newsweek, 48, 49, 50
Numbers research, 30–31

Order clerks, as source of market data, 29–30

Paste-up, 58
Pepto-Bismol, 22
Photography, determining quality of, 62–63, 64–65
Photo retouching, determining quality of, 63
Pica, 58
Point-of-purchase displays, 172–183
  buying, 178–180
  determining need for, 173
  maintaining, 181–183
  obtaining information about, 174–175
  promoting, 180–181
  situations calling for, 173–174
  types of, 175–178
Position of advertisement, 45–47
Postcards, as direct mail pieces, 86
Press party, 105–107
Press proof, 58
Print advertising
  effectiveness of, 109–110
  repetition in, 47
  See also Magazines, advertising
Printing, determining quality of, 61
Product distribution methods, 18–19
Production, 58

INDEX

glossary, 57–59
services, determining quality of, 61–66
Products, new, introducing, 41
Professions market, 17–18
Public relations writers, and news releases, 94–108
circulating release, 107–108
discovering new markets for, 101–102
with photograph, 98
preparing, 95–98
and press parties, 105–107
what to publicize, 98–101
writing when nothing is happening, 102–105
Puns, in advertising, 74

Quality of product, in advertising copy, 74–75

Radio advertising, 109–112
costs, 110
effectiveness of, 110, 111
production of, 110–111
Radio audience, 109
Rand, Paul, 68
Reader's Digest, 51
Redactron Corporation, 100–101
Regional magazines, 47–48
Repetition, in advertising, 47
Representatives, manufacturers', 18–19
Repros, 58
Retail salespeople, as source of market data, 26–28
Retouching, 58
Reverses, 58
ROP (Run of Paper), 110
ROS (Run of Station), 110
Rough, 58

Saddle-stitching, 59

Sales, analyzing, 19–22
Sales letters, 160–171
4-step system for writing, 161–169
length of, 170–171
paper for, 169
personalizing, 169–170
value of color in, 169
Sales meetings, 27, 133–143
importance of, 133–134
planning, 134–137
speakers, 137–139
and speech writing, 139–140
visual aids for speakers at, 140–143
Salespeople
for point-of-purchase display information, 174
sales meetings for, 133–134
and sales promotions, 18
as source of market data, 24–28
Sales presentations, visual, 113–121
Sans serifs, 59
Screens, 59
Seafood Council, 55
Serifs, 59
Silhouette halftone, 59
Silkscreen, 59
Size of advertisement, 45, 70
Space salespeople, as source of market data, 28, 43
Speakers, at sales meetings, 137–139
Speechwriting, for sales meetings, 139–140
Sports Illustrated, 49, 50
Square halftone, 59
Standard Rate and Data, 41, 44, 51
Stuffer, 59
Suggestive selling, in catalogs, 147–148

INDEX

Suppliers' salespeople, as source of market data, 28

Tear sheet, 59
Television, 111
Thompson, J. Walter, 54
Time magazine, 48, 49, 50
Timing, in advertising, 48
Trade associations
  for point-of-purchase display information, 174
  as source of market data, 24
Trade markets, 18
Trade-paper advertising, 39–48
  and new product introductions, 41
  and position of ad, 45–47
  in regionals, 47–48
  selection of publications for, 41–43, 44–45
  and size of ad, 45
  timing in, 48
  value of, 39–40, 41
  vs. direct mail advertising, 40, 41
  and working with space salespeople, 43
Trade publications
  advertising in, 39–48
  as industry statistics source, 22–24
  for point-of-purchase display information, 174

  services of, 23–24
  and space salespeople, 43
Trade shows, 122–132
  attending, 122–123
  carpeting booth, 127
  compiling mailing list at, 127
  displays for booths, 123–126
  distributing literature at, 48, 127–128
  getting people to stop at, 129–130
  giveaways at, 128, 129
  hints, 130–131
  and hospitality suites, 132
  seating at booth, 126–127
  setting up booth, 131–132
TV Guide, 51

U.S. News & World Report, 49, 50
US Steel, 55

Velox, 59
Visual sales presentations, 113–121
  preparing, 114–119
  using effectively, 119–121

Wall Street Journal, 51
Waste, avoiding, 66–67
Westinghouse, 68
Wholesale distributors, 19

ABOUT THE AUTHOR

Cynthia S. Smith is president of C/D Smith Advertising, Inc., in Rye, New York, an advertising agency specializing in small business. She has created and taught a course for New York University entitled *Advertising for the Small and Medium-sized Business*. For the past five years, she has taught seminars on small-budget advertising to executives throughout the country under the aegis of 32 universities, as well as for major corporations and trade associations.